Short Papers on the Church

Hamilton Smith

Scripture Truth Publications

SHORT PAPERS ON THE CHURCH

Revised and reprinted from a series entitled "The Church of God" in "Scripture Truth" magazine, Volume 14, 1922.

Paperback edition first published 1925 by The Central Bible Truth Depot, 5 Rose Street, Paternoster Square, London, E.C. 4.

Re-typeset and transferred to Digital Printing 2008

ISBN: 978-0-901860-80-4 (paperback)

© Copyright 2008 Scripture Truth

A publication of Scripture Truth

All rights reserved. No part of this publication may be reproduced, stored in a retrieval system, or transmitted, in any form or by any means, electronic, mechanical, photocopying, recording or otherwise without prior permission of Scripture Truth Publications.

Scripture quotations, unless otherwise indicated, are taken from The Authorized (King James) Version. Rights in the Authorized Version are vested in the Crown. Reproduced by permission of the Crown's patentee, Cambridge University Press.

Scripture quotations marked "N.Tr." are taken from "The Holy Scriptures, a New Translation from the Original Languages" by J. N. Darby (G Morrish, 1890)

Cover photograph ©iStockphoto.com/iacon (Jeffery Borchert)

Published by Scripture Truth Publications
31-33 Glover Street, Crewe, Cheshire, CW1 3LD

Scripture Truth is an imprint of Central Bible Hammond Trust, a charitable trust

Typesetting by John Rice
Printed and bound by Lightning Source

CONTENTS

1. The Church prophetically announced 5
2. The Church in actual existence 16
3. The Church in the counsels of God 26
4. The Church in the ways of God 35
5. The Church as administered by Paul 44
6. The Church as the house of God according to the mind of God 56
7. The Church as the house of God in the hands of men 64
8. The Church as the body of Christ 71
9. The Church as the body of Christ (continued) . 80
10. The Church in a day of ruin 88

SHORT PAPERS ON THE CHURCH

1.
The Church
Prophetically Announced

MATTHEW 16:1-18; 18:15-20

No Scripture perhaps will give us so deep a sense of the value of the Church to the heart of Christ as that which tells us "Christ also loved the Church and gave Himself for it" (Ephesians 5:25). He did not simply give up His kingdom and throne, with all His earthly rights and glories, *He gave Himself.* If, then, Christ loved the Church with love so great, we may well be at some pains to enquire what is the Church, of whom composed, and why so precious in His sight? What are its privileges, its responsibilities, and what its glorious destiny?

Moreover, the Church is Christ's chief interest on earth—the subject of all God's present dealings. During the period between the coming of the Holy Spirit at Pentecost and the coming of Christ at the rapture, God is not dealing directly with the world, whether Jew or Gentile; He is taking a people out of the world to form the Church for heaven. Without Scriptural thoughts as to the truth of the great mystery concerning Christ and the Church we shall not be able intelligently to enjoy Christian fellowship, take up the service of the Lord, or even fulfil the ordinary duties of life, for when we come to examine the Epistles we shall find that everything in Christianity takes its character from Christ and the Church.

At the outset it may be well to define what we mean when we use the word "Church". It is used in so many different connections that it has become an exceedingly ambiguous term. However, in the original there is no such ambiguity. The Greek word is used one hundred and fifty times in the New Testament. In three instances it is correctly translated "assembly", but in every other instance by this unfortunate word "Church". In Tyndale's translation of the New Testament, the basis of the Authorized Version, the Greek word is rightly translated by the word "congregation"; but in our Authorized Version of 1611, King James, for political reasons, insisted that the ecclesiastical word "Church" should be used, and the Revised Version has unfortunately retained the word. In the New Translation by the late J. N. Darby the word "assembly" is used, and beyond all question this is the simple and proper translation. The context must decide of whom the assembly is composed, but this occasions no real difficulty, for in the New Testament, with the exception of two passages, the word invariably refers to the assembly of God. It may be well to mention that both these exceptions occur in the Acts of the Apostles. In chapter 7:38 the word "Church" is used in reference to Israel. It should be translated "assembly", and of course refers to the congregation of Israel in the wilderness, and has no reference to the assembly of God in the New Testament. The other occurrence is in Acts 19, where the word "assembly" is used three times, and refers, as the context shows, to an assembly of heathen people.

In using, then, the word "Church", it must be always understood to mean an assembly of people, and the assembly of which we speak is the Assembly of God.

With these preliminary remarks we may turn to Matthew 16.

In this important passage we have the first revelation concerning the Church. The Person of Christ is presented as the test of the Jewish system about to pass away, and as the foundation of the new structure that Christ was about to build—His Assembly, the Church.

A great crisis had been reached in the path of the Lord. The most perfect witness to the Messiah had been rendered in the midst of Israel. Signs had been given, miracles had been performed, and prophecies accomplished. The highest moral perfection, in word and life, had been exhibited before men, accompanied by love, grace, and sympathy, that abounded to all, without distinction or limit. Alas! all was in vain. The unbelief, the scorn, the deadly hostility of the leaders increased with every fresh display of grace. At length all is brought to an issue by the great test question, "Whom do men say that I the Son of Man am?" Some said "John the Baptist; some, Elias; and others, Jeremias, or one of the prophets" (verses 13-14).

The reply shows that, in spite of a perfect testimony, men could only advance idle opinions and speculations which left them in hopeless uncertainty. The fact that men are content to speculate about Christ, and willing to remain in uncertainty, is a solemn proof that they have no sense of need on the one hand, and no faith on the other. With a sense of need they would have had discernment, and with faith they would have obtained certainty. Moreover, with all their speculations never once did they approach the truth. This demonstrates the utter incapacity of man, as such, to discern the glory of Christ, even under the most favourable circumstances and in the presence of the Son of God Himself.

In the opening verses of the chapter this unbelief comes to a head. The Pharisees and the Sadducees, who cordially hated one another, are united in their still greater hatred of Christ. The ritualists and the rationalists of the day join hands to tempt the Son of God, and both reveal their utter blindness to the glory of His person by asking for a sign from heaven (verse 1). As one has well said, "Such is unbelief, that it can go into the presence of the full manifestation of God, can gaze at a light brighter than the sun at noonday, and then and there ask God to give a farthing candle." Nothing could bring out more clearly their utter rejection of Christ than this request for a sign. They had rejected Christ and, now, after long patience, are rejected by Christ. They are a wicked and adulterous generation for whom there is only one sign — the sign of Jonas, speaking of imminent judgment. The Lord exposes their character, pronounces their doom, and left them and departed (verse 4). Solemn moment for Israel. The Lord of glory was there; the God that made heaven and earth was in their midst full of grace and truth, but the darkness comprehended Him not. He commenced His ministry of love and grace by coming and dwelling in the land of Nepthalim, so that it could be said, "the people which sat in darkness saw great light and to them which sat in the region and shadow of death light is sprung up." But darkness could not comprehend the light; evil spurned His goodness, and hatred flung back His love. Hence we read those sad, solemn words, "He left them and departed." He left them in the darkness and under the shadow of death.

But does the wickedness of man exhaust the grace of God? Never! On the contrary it becomes the occasion of unfolding the deeper counsels of His heart, and yet greater purposes of grace. The rejection of Israel made way for the revelation of the Church. The moment has come when the first intimation of this great secret, hitherto hidden in God, should be given.

The question that had tested all men is now pressed home upon the disciples, "Whom say ye that I am?" (verse 15). At once Simon Peter replies, "Thou art the Christ, the Son of the living God." How different this reply to the idle opinions of men. Peter's faith may indeed have been weak, for has not the Lord just said, "O ye of little faith", but it was a living faith—a faith that discerned the glory of the Person of Christ, and confessed Him with the utmost certainty.

Immediately following this confession we have *the revelation of the Church*. The Lord lifts the veil that throughout the ages had concealed the eternal counsels of God, and in one brief sentence shows that the glory of His Person as the Son of God "involves depths far beyond an earthly dominion, however glorious".

"Blessed art thou," replies the Lord to Simon Barjona, "for flesh and blood hath not revealed it unto thee, but My Father which is in heaven, and I say also unto thee, that thou art Peter, and upon this rock I will build My Church; and the gates of hades shall not prevail against it" (verses 17-18). Here, then, we have a twofold revelation. First the revelation by the Father. Flesh and blood, as we have seen, could not discern the glory of the Messiah. Only by a revelation from the Father in heaven was it possible for a man on earth to discern that Christ was the Son of the living God,—a title which involves that the Son is

One in whom is life and life-giving power. It has been well said that as the Son of the living God, "He inherits that power of life in God which nothing can overcome or destroy."

But there immediately follows a second revelation—a revelation by the Son, for the Lord says, "And *I also say unto thee.*" The Father had revealed the glory of the Son to Simon Peter, and based on the confession that follows this revelation, the Son also reveals to Peter the great secret, never before made known to man, that upon this rock the Lord was going to build an entirely new structure which He calls "My Assembly". Here, then, we have *the foundation of the Church*. It is raised on a solid and Divine foundation—the Person of the Son of the living God.

Here indeed are truths that flesh and blood could not reveal. When God is communicating the law, Moses and the angels are equal to the occasion; but when it is the glory of the Son, and God's counsels as to the Church, the revelation must, in the first place, come from the Father and the Son. We pass into a region where flesh and blood, as such, can neither communicate nor receive.

Moreover, we see t*he purpose of the Church*. It is brought into existence for the glory and delight of Christ. We learn at the outset that the Church is Christ's. He can say it is "*My* Assembly". The first great thought is, not that Christ is for the Church, but that the Church is for Christ. The Bride, in the Song of Songs, thinking first of her own need, exclaims, "My Beloved is mine"; but at last she is brought to view all from the standpoint of the Bridegroom, and then, with great delight, she can say, "I am my Beloved's, and His desire is toward me." Here, too, in this first great revelation of the Church, all is viewed from Christ as the centre. The Father begins with His glory, and the Church is viewed as for Him—His Assembly.

Furthermore, we learn something of the *structure of the Church*. It is to be built of living stones, Peter being viewed as one of the stones. On that eventful day when Andrew went forth and found his own brother Simon and "brought him to Jesus", the Lord announced that Simon should wear a new name, that he should be called Cephas, which is by interpretation, a stone. Christ as the Son of the living God was the rock on which the Church is built; Peter was a stone, deriving his life from Christ, and destined to be built into this new structure.

We are further instructed as to *the building of the Church*. At the time of this revelation the Church was yet future, for, says the Lord, "I *will* build." Moreover, the work would be wholly Christ's, and therefore, wholly perfect, for the Lord says, "*I* will build." No wood, hay, and stubble would be built into Christ's Assembly—none but living stones would have a place in Christ's building.

Hence the Lord can make this further great statement that against His Church "the gates of Hades shall not prevail."

This speaks of *the stability of the Church*. The gates of Hades signify the power of death wielded by Satan. Through sin man has passed under the dominion of death, a terrific power that lays man's glory in the dust. But in the very world where nothing has withstood the power of death, the Lord foretells that at last He will establish His Church over which the gates of Hades will have no power; and this will be brought to pass because it is based upon the Son of the living God. All else in this world has been based upon Adam—a dying man, and the sons of dying men. But nothing can overcome the power of life in God, whether that life be in God, in Christ, or those to whom He communicates the life. Christ's Assembly is composed of living stones, not dying men. It is built upon Christ, the One who inherits a life that nothing can destroy, and built of stones that possess this life and therefore superior to all the power of death.

The Son of the living God is the everlasting foundation of the Church. Hence there can be no true apprehension of the Church until the glory of the Son is seen and confessed, and the more we apprehend His glory the more we shall appreciate the unique character of the Church.

In this introductory passage we have the revelation of the Church; we are instructed as to the foundation on which the Church is built, the purpose for which it is built, the character of those who compose the building, the One who builds, and the eternal stability of this new and Divine structure.

There is no word as yet of the Body of Christ, or the Bride of Christ. Nothing is said of the exaltation of Christ or the coming of the Spirit. All those great truths so vital to the formation of the Church will be unfolded in due time, but in this first communication "life" is the great thought. Life in the living God, life in the Son, and life communicated to those who compose the Church. Life against which the power of death cannot prevail.

In due time Peter will unfold to us further and precious truths concerning Christ's Assembly. He will tell us how the building grows, as the living stones are drawn to Christ the Living Stone, and for what great end we are built up a spiritual house. John, too, from his island prison will pass on to us a vision of the Assembly when the last stone has been added and the building is displayed in glory as the New Jerusalem. Then, at last, it will be seen that though fashioned in time, Christ's Church is destined for eternity, and though built upon earth it will be displayed in heaven.

There is one other passage in Matthew in which the Lord refers to the Assembly. In chapter 18:15-20 we learn two truths of immense importance to the Assembly. First the Lord instructs us how evil can be excluded from the Assembly, and second how His presence can be secured in the Assembly.

The Assembly is passing through an evil world, and while on earth the flesh remains in those who compose the Assembly; hence on earth offences will come, and even brother may trespass against brother. But the Lord instructs us how to deal with the offender. If he refuses to hear the Assembly, it may even lead to his sin being bound upon him and his exclusion from the company of the Lord's people on earth; and if he repent, his sin can be loosed from him by his reception once again among the Lord's people. This solemn action on earth of binding and loosing—if rightly taken—is ratified in heaven. In the Epistles to the Corinthians we see a solemn example of both actions.

But many difficulties will arise which we have neither wisdom nor power in ourselves to meet. But we have a resource, we can turn to the Father in prayer, and the Lord assures us "That if two of you shall agree on earth as touching anything that they shall ask, it shall be done for them of My Father which is in heaven." Here we have two statements at first sight so surprising that we may well ask, how can these things be? How can it be that acts on earth will be ratified in heaven, and that requests on earth shall be granted by heaven? What is it that makes such things possible? One thing alone, the presence of the Lord in the midst of His people when gathered to His Name. "For," says the Lord, "where two or three are gathered together unto My Name, *there am I in the midst of them.*" He is present to confirm their acts. He is present to guide and answer their prayers .

His presence, however, is only promised to two or three *gathered unto His Name*. What do these words signify? First the promise is given to "two or three", words which, of course, applied to the brightest day of the Church's history, but adapt themselves so blessedly for a day of weakness when the numbers gathered unto His Name in any given place may be reduced to the smallest possible number.

Then the "two or three" do not simply come together, they are *"gathered"* together. This involves a power that gathers. There is something that draws them together; what is it? It is the apprehension of what His Name sets forth, for we gather *unto His Name*, not "in His Name", as we have in our version, which would simply mean that we gather by His authority. His name expresses all that He is, and it is our mutual apprehension of Him in the glory of His Person that draws us together. We are drawn together by what we have found in Him. He is the powerful and all-sufficient bond. There may be great differences in age, social position, education, nationality, intelligence, spiritual growth, and gift, but none of these things form the bond of the Assembly. The Assembly is not a meeting of young people, or of old saints, or like-minded people, but a people who are drawn together by what they have discovered in Christ as set forth in His Name. The Assembly has no other bond, refuses all other bonds, and, gathering together thus, the Lord promises to be in the midst, even if it be but two or three who are thus gathered.

We do not gather to Himself, but to his Name. The passage distinguishes between Himself and His Name. *Gathering to His name supposes His absence, but secures His presence.* In such a gathering He is truly present, not indeed bodily, but in spirit. When on earth He could speak of Himself as the Son of Man which is in heaven; bodily upon earth, but in spirit in heaven. Now He is the Son of Man in heaven, but in spirit on earth in the midst of His people when gathered together unto His Name. Present to give sanction to the exercise of discipline and to give effect to the prayers of His people.

2.
The Church in Actual Existence

ACTS 1-9

In tracing God's thoughts of the Church, as unfolded in His Word, we shall find the early chapters of the Acts carry us a stage in advance of Matthew 16. There the Church is prophetically announced. Here it is formed and seen in actual existence. But it is not yet the subject of the Spirit's teaching; for this the moment had not yet come, nor was the man yet called who was to be the chosen vessel to unfold the mystery of Christ and the Church.

The death of Christ is the basis of all blessing for men, whether for the saints of Old Testament days, for those who compose the Church, or for restored Israel in the age to come. But the formation of the Church awaited two other events of immense import. The risen Christ must ascend as a Man into the glory, and the Holy Spirit—a Divine Person—must come to earth. The Man in the glory and the Holy Spirit abiding on earth, are the two great distinguishing facts of the Christian period. They had no existence in the ages that are past, and they will not mark the ages that are to come; they give the entire character to the present moment.

In the first chapter of the Acts we see the fulfilment of the first great event. Here the disciples receive the last directions from the risen Lord, and "while they beheld, He was taken up; and a cloud received Him out of their sight." Christ as a Man was received up into the glory. Of course, in so speaking we must never forget that He is a Divine Person "over all, God blessed for ever." But still it is as Man He ascends to heaven, and as the Son of Man He is seen in heaven by the martyr Stephen.

In the second chapter of the Acts we get the fulfilment of the second great event. The Holy Ghost is received on earth according to that word in John 7:39, which connects His coming with the glory of Christ. The disciples were "all together in one place" waiting, according to the Lord's word, for the baptism of the Holy Spirit. While waiting, the Holy Spirit came "from heaven" and filled all the house where they were sitting; and not only so, but each individual was filled with the Holy Spirit. Thus by one Spirit they were "all baptized into one body" (1 Corinthians 12:13). Here, then, the "one body" became an actual fact: that body of which Christ is the Head in heaven, and believers the members on earth. The fact was not yet revealed, and could hardly be, as the body is composed of Jewish and Gentile believers, and hence the revelation of the truth was not given until the Gentile believers had been baptized into the body by the Holy Spirit (*see* Acts 10; 11:16).

Following upon the baptism of the Spirit, a great number of Jews and proselytes were convicted, believed in Christ, were baptized, received the forgiveness of sins and the gift of the Holy Spirit. Further, we read, "the same day there were added about three thousand souls" (Acts 2:41). Then the last verse of the chapter tells us who added them, and to what they were added. It was the Lord Himself who added them, and it was to the Church they were added. For the first time we are permitted to see the Lord forming His Church according to His own prophetic announcement in Matthew 16. "I will build My Church." The closing words of the verse, "such as should be saved", do not imply that they were unbelievers, or that they were added in order to be saved. The nation having rejected Christ was going on to judgment, but those who believed and were baptized would be saved from that judgment, and such the Lord added to the Church. They were added to the Lord before they were added to the Church. To insist upon this is of the greatest importance, because Rome, and those who follow Rome, "attach salvation to being of the Church, instead of making the Church the assembly of those who are saved". Only believers in the beginning of the chapter were formed into the Church by the baptism of the Holy Spirit, and only believers at the end of the chapter were added to the Church by the Lord.

Here, then, the Church is seen in actual existence. "All that believed were together" (Acts 2:44). We thus see the fulfilment of that word spoken by Caiaphas concerning Christ when he said, "He should gather together in one the children of God that were scattered abroad." It has been truly said, "There were indeed children of God before this moment, but they were scattered abroad, they were isolated. Christ by His death was to *gather them together*, not merely to save them, so that they might be together in heaven (since they were children of God that was already done), but He was to gather them together in one." This was something entirely new upon the earth. It was no new thing for children of God to exist on the earth. It was no new thing that such were journeying on to heaven. That was true in Enoch's day, and Job's day, and throughout the days of old, however dimly it was known. But that the children of God should be *gathered together in one* was an entirely new thing. And this is the truth that the people of God are still so slow to apprehend. We think of ourselves as isolated saints, as if we lived before the Cross. Being saved we are apt to think that it is left to us, according to the best of our ability, to choose what "church" we shall join, or whether we shall join any at all. But in this thought we fail to see that already, if we have come to the Lord, He has added us to the Church, and hence there can be no question of remaining in isolation on the one hand, or of joining a church on the other. The very thought of joining *a* church betrays ignorance of the truth of *the* Church.

Moreover, not only were the saints gathered together in one, but being gathered together God makes ample provision that they might continue together in a visible unity.

First, we have *"the apostles' teaching"*, by which the saints were led into all the truth of God and instructed in the mind of God as to their pathway on earth. This instruction, given orally at first, was later on, secured to the saints for all time in the inspired Epistles.

Second, flowing from the apostles' teaching, we have *"the apostles' fellowship"*. This, as we know, is the fellowship into which all Christians are called—the fellowship of God's Son, Jesus Christ our Lord. The Son of God is the centre and object of this fellowship.

Third, the apostles' fellowship leads to *"the breaking of bread"*, the formal and highest expression of fellowship; that which calls to remembrance the death of Christ by which the children of God have been entirely separated from the world and gathered together in one.

Lastly, *"prayer"*, by which, as saints, we are kept in the attitude of dependence upon God, recognizing that His grace is available for us, and that we constantly need to come boldly to the throne of grace that we may receive mercy, and find grace to help in time of need.

Alas! God's provision has been almost wholly neglected, and hence the divided and scattered condition of God's people. Christendom has largely set aside the apostles' doctrine by its own tradition; has formed "fellowships" around gifted men, or particular views, instead of the Son of God; has perverted the breaking of bread from a supper of remembrance to a ceremonial means of grace, and turned prayer into mere formality. However, in the early days of the Acts the believers "continued steadfastly" in the apostles' doctrine, and fellowship, and breaking of bread, and prayer; and as long as they so continued they remained together in a visible unity.

We have thus seen in the second chapter of the Acts how the Lord Himself builds His Church with living stones upon the Rock. But all this takes place on earth; there is as yet no hint of the heavenly character of the Assembly, or of its glorious destiny in the counsels of God. There is not a word so far of the union of the Body on earth with the Head in heaven. "Union" is still a secret to be unfolded in due time, but what is manifested in these early chapters of the Acts is "unity". Not necessarily *a material unity*, but *a moral unity*, marked by gladness and singleness of heart. There remained one event to be fulfilled before the full heavenly character and calling of the Church could be revealed. Israel's cup of guilt must be filled to the brim. Already the nation had rejected and crucified their Messiah; but now the Holy Spirit had come, with the last offer to the guilty nation. Will they resist the Spirit as they had already rejected the Messiah?

When the Lord ascended, as recorded in Acts 1, the disciples "looked steadfastly toward Heaven as He went up." Immediately two angels stood by them, which said, "Why stand ye gazing up into heaven? this same Jesus, which is taken up from you into heaven, shall so come in like manner." The angels turn their gaze from heaven, whence Christ had gone, towards the earth to which He will come. At first we might wonder at this. Surely it was a right thing to look up to heaven where Christ is? Yes, in due season it will be right, but the moment had not yet come to look up. And as we listen to Peter preaching to the nation we can understand why the disciples' thoughts were to linger for a while on earth. For says Peter to the guilty nation, "Repent ye, therefore, and be converted, that your sins may be blotted out, when the times of refreshing shall come from the presence of the Lord, and *He shall send Jesus Christ*, which before was preached unto you" (Acts 3:19-20). This was the final message in grace to the guilty nation proclaimed by the Holy Spirit come down from the ascended Christ. If they will repent, Jesus will come back to earth. In result they utterly refuse this testimony of the Holy Spirit. They had been the betrayers and murderers of their own Messiah. The Holy Spirit (not having taken a body) they could not murder, but they can murder the man that is filled with the Holy Spirit, and this they do by stoning the witness Stephen.

The rejection by the nation of this final offer of grace brings about an entire change in the dispensation. Henceforth it is all over with them, and the centre of all God's dealings passes from earth to heaven. In harmony with this change Stephen, being filled with the Holy

Ghost, looked up steadfastly into heaven, and no angel stands by to inquire why he looks up. God's time has come for His people to look away from earth to heaven. And not only he looks up, but his happy spirit is received up. The first of the long line of martyrs is received into heaven. Now God's people no longer belong to earth from which Christ has been rejected, but to heaven where Christ has been received. Heaven is their home, and Christ is there to receive them into that home. If the world will not have Christ it is no place for His people, and if heaven has received Christ then a new place is opened for His people, and into that new place He receives them.

The seventh chapter of the Acts is a great turning-point in the ways of God. From the moment the testimony of Stephen is rejected the great characteristics of the dispensation come prominently to the fore. In the closing scene of this chapter everyone, and everything stands revealed according to the true character of the Christian dispensation. *The guilty nation of Israel* is seen in its absolute rejection of Christ and its inveterate resistance to the Holy Spirit. *The world* is seen in its true character as the rejector of Christ and the persecutor of His saints. *Heaven* is seen flung open to disclose Christ in the glory, for the reception of the saints. *Christ* is seen as the Man in the glory supporting His tried saints on earth and receiving them to heaven as they fall asleep. *The Holy Spirit* is seen as a Divine Person on earth, filling a man on earth and leading him to look up steadfastly to Christ in heaven. And lastly, this Spirit-filled *saint* is presented as a man on earth drawing all his resources from the Man in the glory, and so doing becoming changed into His likeness from glory to glory, in such fashion that, like his Master, he prays for his murderers and commits his spirit to the

THE CHURCH IN ACTUAL EXISTENCE

Lord. So that *as a man on earth is supported by the Man in the glory, the Man in the glory is represented by a man on earth.* Having fought the fight and finished his course, Stephen's happy spirit departs to be with Christ, while his poor battered body falls asleep to await a glorious resurrection.

Ever since the stoning of Stephen, the world has been true to its character. It rejected Christ then, it persecuted the saints then, it has done so ever since in different measures and degrees. It may be religious—it was so then, and it is so now—but religion does not change its character. Indeed, the greater the world's profession of religion, the more intense its hatred and the more relentless its persecution of the saints. Let history bear witness to its unchanging hostility to Christ and His people. Heaven, too, has not changed its attitude to God's people. It was open then, it is open still; and through that open door we can still look into the glory where Jesus is, and the love of Christ still streams down upon His saints. Then truly with Christ there is no change. We can look up and say, "Thou remainest" and "Thou art the same." All the grace and power and wisdom of the Man in the glory are still as available for the support of His people as when Stephen was so blessedly sustained in his martyrdom. With the Holy Spirit, too, there is no change. He came from Christ in the glory to lead us to Christ in the glory. And this is still the way He takes. But, alas, how believers have changed. How little we have remained true to our character as saints. How much we have grieved the Spirit, and thus, instead of looking steadfastly to heaven, we have looked to earth. We have become earthly, if not worldly. Consequently the support of the Lord has been little received and the power of the Spirit but little manifested, so that we have been but poor representatives of the Man in the glory.

But in spite of all failure, the picture in Acts 7 remains in all its excellent beauty to recall our hearts to the true character of the dispensation. But it does more; it prepares the way for the ministry of Paul with its rich unfolding of the Church as the one Body with Christ the risen Head in heaven.

In the history of Stephen we surely learn that the disciples of the risen Christ belong to heaven. But in the story of Paul's conversion in Acts 9 we learn, not only that the saints belong to heaven, but that the saints on earth are united to Christ in heaven. As Saul journeyed on his way to Damascus "breathing out threatenings and slaughter against the disciples of the Lord", he was struck to the ground by a light from heaven and heard the voice of Christ from the glory saying unto him, "Saul, Saul, why persecutest thou *Me*?" The voice did not say, "Mine", nor even "us", but "Me". "Mine" would imply a company of people that belong to Christ; true indeed, but not all the truth. "Us" would imply a company of people associated with Christ; also true, but not the full truth. "Me" involves a company of people *in union with Christ*, and in such intimate fashion that to touch them is to touch Christ.

The martyrdom of Stephen and the persecution that follows presents the world in its true character as a persecutor of the saints; but at the conversion of Saul we learn the further truth that in persecuting the saints the world is persecuting Christ. The Church is one with Christ in heaven and He is persecuted in His members. This, as it has been said, is "the strongest expression of our union with Him—that He considers the feeblest member

THE CHURCH IN ACTUAL EXISTENCE

of His body as part of Himself." In Acts 2 and 4 the saints were gathered together with "one heart" and "one soul" presenting a beautiful expression of *unity*; but here is disclosed the deeper truth of their intimate *union* with Christ, their exalted Head in heaven, and with one another as members of His body on earth.

Israel, having crucified the Messiah, rejected Christ in the glory, and resisted the Holy Spirit on earth, are entirely set aside for the time being, while the Church, formed on earth but destined for glory, becomes the witness for God in the world. Paul was the chosen vessel to unfold by Divine teaching in his Epistles the great truths concerning Christ and the Church.

3.
The Church
in the Counsels of God

EPHESIANS 1; 2:1-10

In Matthew 16 we have the prophetic announcement of the Church by the Lord Himself; in the Acts we have the historical account of the formation of the Church through the ministry of the apostles; and in the Epistles the Divine teaching as to the Church by the Holy Spirit. The Epistle to the Ephesians presents this teaching in its greatest fulness.

Chapter 1 presents God's counsels in regard to Christ and the Church. We are carried back before the foundation of the world to trace the source of all our blessings in God's eternal purpose: we are transported to the fulness of times, there to see the inheritance of glory when all God's counsels will be fulfilled. In chapter 2:1-10 we have God's work in us, in view of His counsels for us, whereby He quickens dead souls, raises them up together with Christ, and seats them in Christ in the heavenlies.

In chapter 2:11-22 we have God's ways with us in time to bring about His counsels for us in eternity. There is what

THE CHURCH IN THE COUNSELS OF GOD

God has purposed *for us*, what God works *in us*, and what God does *with us*. He works in us that we might be quickened together with Christ; He works with us that we might be brought together in one body, fitly framed together into a holy temple in the Lord, and builded together for an habitation of God through the Spirit.

We can, however, readily understand that the epistle must of necessity commence with unfolding the purpose of God; for unless we know His purposes for eternity we shall not understand His ways in time. We might well be puzzled by the way a parent trains his child until we learn the parent's ultimate purpose for the child. Confining then our thoughts to the early part of the epistle (1; 2:1-10) we see the Church presented in connection with the counsels and work of God. Man's work and man's responsibilities have no place in this passage. All is counselled by God, and all is carried out by God: and, being of God, all is perfect.

Verses 3-7 unfold the counsels of God for His saints individually—those who compose the Church. In this great passage we see *the character* of our blessings, *the source* of our blessings, *the end* God has in view, and *the means* by which that end is reached.

As to the character of our blessings, it is important to remember that they are spiritual, and heavenly, and in Christ, for we are so prone to look for blessings that are material, and earthly, and in connection with Adam. The realization of the true character of our blessings would have an immense effect upon our testimony. What is the aim of the great mass of so-called ministry to-day? Is it not, in the main, to make believers moral rather than spiritual, to improve their earthly position rather than call them out of the world for heaven, and to improve the first man rather than lead into the new position in Christ. God forms our character and testimony by instructing us in the true character of our blessings and leading us into the enjoyment of them.

As to the source of all our blessings we read, "the God and Father of our Lord Jesus Christ … hath chosen us in Him before the foundation of the world." All our blessings have their source in the counsels of the Father's heart. We discover that His heart was set upon us before the foundation of the world. And He delights that we should know it; and loving the Father, we count it one of our choicest privileges that He should have revealed to us the secrets of His heart. Chosen in Him before the foundation of the world involves a choice that is independent of the scene of creation. Hence God's purpose for us cannot depend upon anything that we have done or can do. We find ourselves in a world of sorrow and trial, of opposition and persecution, but God's purpose cannot be altered by anything we are called to pass through in time. The devil would fain use the difficulties of the way to raise in our hearts distrust of God and to call in question the reality of His love. But here we are permitted to see that the love of the Father is behind all, and that, before the foundation of the world, He set His love upon us in view of our eternal blessing when the world shall be no more. How this steadies the soul in its journey through the world, for nothing that takes place in the ways of God in time can touch the counsels of love that were settled in eternity and for eternity.

Moreover, we are not only carried back before the foundation of the world to find the source of all our blessing in the heart of God, but we are carried on in spirit to view the end of all God's counsels in glory. Thus we learn that God had purposed to have the saints before Him in a condition that is suited to Him: "Holy and without blame before Him in love". Holy in character, without blame in conduct, and in love as to nature. Nothing less would suit the heart of God; for if God is to have a people before Him in a condition suited *to Him*, it must be in a condition in which they are *like Him*. Only that which is like God is suited to God. God is holy in character, blameless in all His ways, and love in His nature. And in this condition He has purposed to have us so that He can delight in us and we can delight in Him. Nothing less would suit His heart, and nothing less would make us happy in His presence. No question as to character, or conduct, or nature will ever be raised in that scene to mar our joy in God or His satisfaction in us. And what will be accomplished in its fulness then is wrought in our souls by the Spirit now. If in the power of the Spirit, we shall seek to answer down here to what we shall be in perfection up there.

Furthermore, not only are we chosen to be in a condition suited to God, but we are predestined to enjoy the relationship of sons before the Father. Angels, doubtless, will be before God in a condition suited to God, but they are there in the position of servants. We are brought into the relationship of sons. This is the special privilege to which we are predestined according to the good pleasure of His will, to the praise of the glory of His grace.

Moreover, in view of the accomplishment of God's purpose, we must be redeemed and have the forgiveness of sins through the blood of Christ, according to the riches of His grace. The Apostle has connected predestination with "the glory of His grace", now he connects redemption with "the riches of His grace". Our great need is met by the riches of His grace, but the glory of His grace does more, it takes us into favour and gives us the place of sons.

Meeting the prodigal's need shows how rich the resources of grace in the Father's home; but giving him the place of son, displayed the glory of the grace in the Father's heart. In the epistle to the Romans the death of Christ is fully developed in meeting all our responsibilities, and hence there the apostle exclaims "O the depth of the *riches* both of the wisdom and knowledge of God." In Ephesians the apostle passes beyond our responsibilities to unfold our privileges, hence we have, not only the riches of His grace, but the *glory* of His grace.

Having then, in the first seven verses, unfolded the counsels of the Father's heart concerning His people, the apostle passes on to fresh wonders. He discloses to us the Father's secret will concerning Christ. He has satisfied our hearts by unfolding the purposes of love, He has given the conscience rest by the work of redemption, and thus set free, we are able to enter into God's thoughts concerning Christ and the Church.

God would have us to know the mystery of His will, according to His good pleasure which He hath purposed in Himself for the administration of the fulness of times. What does this word "mystery" mean? Is it something that we cannot understand, or that is mysterious or puzzling? Far from it. In Scripture a mystery is a secret that cannot possibly be known until revealed by God, and when revealed can only be known by the initiated. This mystery is according to His good pleasure; it is a secret that delights His heart, for it concerns Christ. Do we say that we are not interested in mysteries, that we leave these deep things to others? Surely not, for this would mean that we are content to know what God has in His heart for us, without any concern as to what God has in His heart for Christ.

Here the mystery has reference to the "fulness of times" when God will have everything administered according to His mind: when everything that God has instituted at other times, and which has so utterly failed in the hands of men, will be administered in all its fulness under Christ. Government and priesthood and royalty were instituted by God in other days, only to break down because committed to man's responsibility. But the time is coming when they will all be seen in perfection and fulness. This will be brought about by heading up all things in Christ, both which are in heaven and which are on earth. At present Christ is hidden; but when He comes forth in glory, all the confusion, the sorrow and disorder of this world will be past. Satan's reign will be ended, the time of Israel's blindness will be over, the godless rule of the Gentile nations will be closed, the groan of creation will be hushed, and the curse will be removed. All will be brought about, not by the spread of the Gospel, as some vainly imagine, or by anything that man can accomplish, but by Christ alone. When He sets up His throne—when He reigns—all will be administered to the good pleasure of God.

The Old Testament abundantly foretells "the sufferings of Christ and the glories that should follow", which glories, though they reach to the utmost bounds of earth, are still earthly and not heavenly. This is no secret or mystery, on the contrary the prophets are full of glowing descriptions of the earthly kingdom. When, however, we come to the New Testament, God unfolds to us the great secret, that Christ's dominion will stretch immeasurably beyond the limits of earth; that as a Man, Christ will have dominion not only "from sea to sea, and from the river to the ends of the earth", but over the whole vast universe of God to the utmost bounds of creation; that He should be set far above all principality and power and might, and dominion, and every name that is named, not only in this world, but also in that which is to come; yea more that all things in heaven and earth will be united under Christ as Head.

God has abounded to us in all wisdom and intelligence in thus making known to us not only His purpose for His people, but the secrets of His heart for Christ; not only His purpose for earth but His secrets concerning the whole universe. The heavens are now severed from the earth, but it will not always be so. God has purposed to unite heaven and earth under Christ as Man. This is the mystery of His will, but even so it is not the whole mystery. For the mystery concerns "Christ and the Church" (Ephesians 5:32). Not Christ alone, nor the Church alone, but Christ and the Church. This leads us on to the most amazing part of the mystery; that in the day of His universal dominion, Christ will have a vast company of people—saved from the wreck and ruin of this fallen world—made like to Himself as the result of His own work, united to Him by the Holy Spirit, to share with Him in all the glory of His universal sway as His body and His bride.

The remaining portion of this chapter brings before us this further truth. The apostle continues "in whom also we have obtained an inheritance." In verses 11 and 12 he speaks of the Jewish believers, in verse 13, of the Gentile believers, and in verse 14, in speaking of "*our* inheritance" he refers to both Jewish and Gentile believers together.

Thus, to use the words of another, this great mystery is "Christ and the Church united in heavenly blessedness and dominion over everything that God has made."

Christ will reign over Israel, over the Gentiles, over the whole Universe, but never is it said that He will reign over the Church. Christ, indeed, will ever be supreme, but to the praise of His glory the Church will reign *with Him*.

This is made more abundantly plain by the apostle's prayer with which the chapter closes. Having unfolded the hope of the calling in verses 3 to 7, and the inheritance in verses 8 to 14, the apostle now prays that we may know these things, and moreover that we may know the greatness of the power to usward that will bring these glorious truths to fruition. This power has been set forth in raising Christ from the dead and setting Him "above all" and putting "all things under His feet". But while it is given to Christ as Man to be Head over all, He is Head *to* the Church which is His body, the fulness of Him that filleth all things. Here the Church is viewed as the body of Christ, not in the ways of God on earth, but according to the counsels of God in glory.

In the beginning of the chapter we have the unfolding of the counsels of God for the individuals who compose the Church, in the end of the chapter the counsels of God for the Church, as a whole, under the figure of a body. We are taken on to a time when the body, complete in glory, will be united to the Head in His dominion over all things.

Adam and Eve furnish a type of Christ and the Church. Eve was not directly set in dominion over this lower world, but Adam was. It is true God said unto them "Be fruitful … and have dominion", but actually Adam was set in dominion before Eve was formed. The animal creation was brought to Adam to name; he was in relation with all as head over all, and by association with Adam, Eve shared in his dominion.

So the Church, by association with Christ, will share in His universal dominion over all creation. And just as Eve was said to be a helpmeet for Adam—his counterpart—

so the Church is said to be the fulness of Him that filleth all in all. Apart from the Church, Christ would lack His fulness. As one has said, "As Son of God, He, of course, requires nothing to complete His glory; but as Man He does. He would no more be complete in His resurrection glory without the Church, than Adam would have been without Eve."

4.
The Church in the Ways of God

EPHESIANS 2:11-22

In the first part of the Epistle to the Ephesians, chapters 1 and 2:1-10, the Church is presented in relation to Christ in glory, according to the counsels of God. This prepares the way for a very different view of the Church—its formation and testimony on earth according to the ways of God.

There is a vast difference between the counsels of God for glory and the ways of God on earth. Seizing this distinction, we shall see that not only has the Church a glorious destiny as united to Christ in heaven, according to the eternal purpose of God, but that it also has an existence on earth, and a great place in the ways of God here below. It is this aspect of the Church that comes before us in Ephesians 2 verses 11 to 22.

In order that we may understand this very important aspect of the Church, the Apostle reminds us of the distinct position held by Israel in the times before the Cross. At that time there existed a very sharp distinction between

Jew and Gentile. In the ways of God on earth the Jew enjoyed a place of privilege to which the Gentile was an entire stranger. Israel formed an earthly commonwealth, with earthly promises and earthly hopes. They were in outward relationship with God. Their religious worship, their political organization, their daily pursuits, their domestic affairs, all, from the highest act of worship to the smallest detail of life, were regulated by the ordinances of God. This was an immense privilege in which the Gentiles, as such, had no part. It was not that the Jews were any better than the Gentiles, for, in the sight of God, the great mass of the Jews were as bad as the Gentiles, and some even worse; and on the other hand, there were individual Gentiles who were truly converted men, such, for instance, as Job. But in the ways of God upon earth He separated Israel from the Gentiles, and gave them a place of special outward privilege; for even if unconverted (as indeed was the case with the mass) it was an immense privilege to have all their affairs regulated according to the perfect wisdom of God. The Gentiles had no such position in the world. They enjoyed no public recognition of God. Their affairs were not regulated by the ordinances of God. And the very ordinances that regulated the life of the Jew sternly kept Jew and Gentile apart.

Thus the Jew had a place on earth of outward nearness to God, while the Gentile was outwardly far off with no recognized connection with God in the world.

But Israel entirely failed to answer to their privileges. They turned from Jehovah to idols. The commandments and ordinances of God, which gave them their unique position, they wholly disregarded. Finally, they crucified their Messiah and resisted the Holy Spirit. As a result they have, for the time being, lost their special place of privilege on the earth, have been dispossessed of their land and scattered among the nations.

This setting aside of Israel prepares the way for the marvellous change that has taken place in the ways of God on earth. The vivid glimpse into the past given by the Spirit of God in verses 11 and 12 only makes the contrast more striking, for, following upon the rejection of Israel, God, in the pursuit of His ways, has brought to light the Church and thus set up an entirely new circle of blessing, wholly outside the Jewish and Gentile circles.

This new departure becomes the occasion of the grace of God flowing out in a very special way to the Gentile. The call goes out to the Gentile; not, indeed, that the Jew is excluded from the new circle of blessing, for, as we shall see, the Church is composed of believers from among both Jews and Gentiles.

But if the Gentile is to be brought into the inestimable privileges and blessings of the new circle—if the Gentile is to have part in the Church—it must be on a righteous ground. Hence the Cross is at once brought in (verse 13). The Cross has already been alluded to in chapter 1 in connection with the fulfilment of the counsels of God. Here in chapter 2 the Cross is referred to in connection with the ways of God on earth. By the blood of Christ sinners of the Gentiles are made nigh to God, being brought from the place of distance in which sin had put them, into a place of nearness. Not a mere outward nearness, by means of ordinances and ceremonies, but a vital nearness that is only fully expressed in Christ Himself risen from the dead and appearing before the face of God for us. Hence it is said, "*in Christ Jesus* ye ... are made nigh by the blood of Christ." Our sins put us afar off, but not only does the precious blood wash away our sins, it does more, infinitely more, it makes us nigh. The blood of Christ declares the enormity of the sin which demanded such a price, proclaims the holiness of God that could be satisfied with no less a price, and reveals the infinite love that could pay the price.

But this, however necessary for the formation of the Church, does not in itself constitute the Church. The Church is not simply a number of individuals "made nigh", for this will be true of every blood-bought saint of every age. There is more needed; not only must individuals be *"made nigh"*, but Jewish and Gentile believers must be *"made both one"* (verse 14). This, too, the cross of Christ has accomplished. There Christ broke down the barrier between Jew and Gentile. The enmity between Jew and Gentile was caused by the ordinances which excluded the Gentile from having part in them. By these ordinances the Jew could approach God in an outward way while the Gentile could not. But in the cross Christ has entirely abolished the law of ordinances as a means of approach to God, and made a new way of approach by His blood. The Jew who approaches God on the ground of the blood has done with the Jewish ordinances. The Gentile comes out of his distance from God; the Jew out of his dispensational nearness, and both are made one in the enjoyment of a common blessing before God never before possessed by either. The Gentile believers are not raised to the level of Jewish privileges. The Jews are not degraded to the Gentile level. Both are brought on to an entirely new ground on an immeasurably higher plane.

But even this does not express the full truth of the Church. Had the Apostle stopped here we should indeed have seen that believers are made nigh by the blood and made one as having all enmity removed, but we might have been left with the thought that we are made one company in happy unity. And that indeed is blessedly true, but, even so, far short of the full truth as to the Church. So the Apostle proceeds further and tells us that we are not only *"made nigh"*, and not only *"made both one"*, but that we are made *"one new man"* (verse 15), "one body" (verse 16), indwelt by "one Spirit", by whom we have access to the Father (verse 18). This, indeed, presents the full truth of the Church—the body of Christ—that in the ways of God is being formed on earth.

God is not only saving souls from Jews and Gentiles on the ground of the blood. Not only is He gathering such together in *unity*, but He is forming them into one New Man of which Christ is the glorious Head, believers are the members of the body, and the Holy Spirit the uniting power. This is far more than unity; it is *union*. The Church is not simply a company of believers in happy unity, but a company of people who are members of Christ and of one another in intimate union. And the New Man is not merely new in point of time, but is of an entirely new order. Before the Cross, as we have seen, there were two men, Jew and Gentile, hating one another and at enmity with God. Now in the marvellous ways of God "One New Man" has come into being. A *New* Man which embraces every saint on earth united by One Spirit to Christ the risen and exalted Head.

Connected with the formation of the Church of God on earth the Apostle refers to three great truths, reconciliation to God, the preaching of peace to sinners, and access to the Father on the part of saints.

First, both Jew and Gentile are reconciled to God in one body (verse 16). God was not content that the Gentile should remain at a distance from Him, or that the Jew should be in a place of mere outward nearness, but in actual distance as great as the Gentile. Nor was God content that Jew and Gentile should remain at a distance from one another. Therefore in the Cross He has so wondrously wrought that both have been brought nigh to Him, and both have been brought nigh to one another, formed into one body upon which God can look with complacency. The Cross has slain the enmity between Jew and Gentile believers, as also that which once stood between both and God. Nothing could more perfectly express the entire removal of the enmity than the fact of the Jewish and Gentile believers being formed into "one body". It is not said in this verse "One New Man", because that includes Christ the Head, and no thought of reconciliation can be connected with Christ. It is those who compose the body who need reconciliation, not the One who is the Head.

The second great truth is that the gospel of peace is preached to the Gentiles who were far off, and to the Jews, who were dispensationally near. We can well understand the introduction of the preaching into a passage that shows how the Church is formed on earth. Without the Cross there could be no preaching, and without the preaching there would be no Church. Christ is looked at as the Preacher, though the gospel He preaches is proclaimed instrumentally through others. We read of the disciples that "they went forth and preached everywhere, *the Lord working with them*" (Mark 16:20).

There is a third truth of great blessedness. By one Spirit we both (Jew and Gentile) have access to the Father. The distance is not only removed on God's side, but it is also removed on our side. By the work of Christ on the cross God can draw nigh to us, preaching peace, and by the work of the Spirit in us we can draw nigh to the Father. The Cross gives us our title to draw nigh, the Spirit enables us to use our title and practically draw nigh to the Father. But if access is by the Spirit, then clearly there is no room for the flesh. The Spirit excludes the flesh in every form. It is not by buildings, or ritual, or organs, or choirs, or a special class of men, that we gain access to the Father. Nay, all these fleshly means that so impress the natural man will most effectually bar all access to the Father. It is by the Spirit, but more, it is by "one Spirit", and therefore in the Father's presence all is of one accord. As we rightly sing,

"*No jarring note shall there discordant sound.*"

Do not flat and low assembly meetings arise from the solemn fact that we have dared to bring into the presence of the Lord unjudged flesh? Or again, meetings otherwise happy are suddenly jarred by an unsuitable hymn, or unseasonable ministry, because we are not all led by *"one Spirit"*. Do we speak thus to fill any with a morbid dread of introducing that which would quench the Spirit, and thus silence them? On the contrary, let such remember that their silence may be as much an intrusion of the flesh as the forwardness of others. Let all judge themselves and so come into the presence of the Lord. Then, indeed, the Spirit will be free to give access to the Father.

Thus far we have viewed the Church as the body of Christ; but in the ways of God on earth the Church is viewed in other aspects, two of which are brought before us in the closing verses of the chapter (verses 19-22). First, the Church is viewed as growing unto "an holy temple in the Lord"; secondly, as "an habitation of God".

In the first aspect the Church is likened to a progressive building growing unto a holy temple in the Lord. The apostles and prophets form the foundation, Christ Himself being the chief corner stone. Throughout the

Christian dispensation believers are being added stone by stone until the last believer is built in and the completed building displayed in glory. This is the building of which the Lord says in Matthew 16, "I will build My Church, and the gates of hades shall not prevail against it." Christ is the builder, not man, hence all is perfect, and none but living stones form part of this holy structure. Peter gives us the spiritual significance of this building when he tells us that the living stones are built up a spiritual house "to offer up spiritual sacrifices to God", on the one hand, and to "show forth the excellencies" of God, on the other (1 Peter 2:5, 9). In Revelation 21 John sees a vision of the completed building descending out of heaven from God, and radiant with the glory of God. Then, indeed, from that glorious building unceasing sacrifices of praise will rise up to God, and a perfect testimony to the excellencies of God will flow forth to man.

Then the Apostle, still using the figure of a building, presents another aspect of the Church (verse 22). He views the saints as no longer being built into a growing temple, but as forming a house already complete for an habitation of God through the Spirit. All believers on earth at any given moment are looked at as forming the habitation of God. But the Apostle does not merely say "ye are an habitation", but "ye are *builded together* for an habitation". That is, this habitation is formed of Jewish and Gentile believers "builded together". The dwelling place of God is marked by light and love; therefore, when the Apostle comes to the practical part of the Epistle he exhorts us as dear children to "walk in love", and to "walk as children of light" (Ephesians 5:2, 8). The house of God is thus a place of blessing and testimony: a place where the saints are blessed with the favour and love of God; and, thus blessed, they become a testimony to the world around. In

Ephesians the habitation of God is presented according to the mind of God, and therefore only what is real is contemplated. Other Scriptures will show, also how in our hands the habitation has become corrupted until at last we read that judgment must begin at the house of God.

Thus in this chapter we have a threefold presentation of the Church.

1st. The Church is viewed as the body of Christ, composed of Jewish and Gentile believers united to Christ in glory, thus forming one New Man for the display of all that Christ is as the risen Man, Head over all things. For let us remember that the Church is not only "one body", but it is "His body", as we read, "the Church which is His body". And as His body it is "the fulness of Him". It is filled with all that He is in order to express all that He is. The Church—His body—is to be the expression of His mind, just as our bodies give expression to what is in our minds.

2nd. Then the Church is a growing temple composed of all the saints of the whole Christian period, wherein sacrifices of praise ascend to God and the excellencies of God are displayed to men.

3rd. Lastly, the Church is viewed as a complete building on earth, composed of all the saints at any given moment, forming the habitation of God for blessing to His people and testimony to the world.

5.
The Church as Administered by Paul

EPHESIANS 3

We have viewed the Church according to the counsels of God in the first portion of the Epistle to the Ephesians (1; 2:1-10). We have also seen the Church in the ways of God on earth in chapter 2:11-22. Coming now to the third chapter, we have the Church presented in connection with the administration of Paul. The whole chapter is a parenthesis. Chapter 2 presents the doctrine of the Church; chapter 4, the practical exhortations based upon the doctrine. Between the doctrine and the exhortations we have this important digression in which the Holy Spirit presents the special administration, or service, committed to Paul in connection with the truth of the Church.

In connection with this service we learn that it was the insistence upon the truth of the Church that brought the Apostle within the walls of a prison. This great truth aroused the special hatred and hostility of the Jew inasmuch as it not only viewed Jew and Gentile in the same position before God —dead in trespasses and sins—but it entirely refused to exalt the Jew to a place of blessing above the Gentile.

We are then informed by what means the Apostle acquired his knowledge of the truth of the mystery. It was not through communications from men, but by a direct revelation from God: "By revelation He made known unto me the mystery." This meets a great difficulty that arises in connection with the truth of the mystery. When Paul preached the Gospel in the Jewish synagogues, he invariably appealed to the Scriptures (*see* Acts 13:27, 29, 32-35, 47; 17:2, etc.), and the Jews of Berea are expressly commended inasmuch as they searched the Scripture to see if the word preached by Paul was in accord with it. But directly the Apostle ministered the truth of the Church he could no longer appeal to the Old Testament for confirmation. It would be useless for his hearers to search the Scriptures to see if these things were so. The unbelief of the Jew made it difficult for him to accept many truths that were in their Scriptures, even as Nicodemus failed to grasp the truth of new birth, but to accept something that was not there, something, too, which set aside the whole Jewish system that was there, and which had existed with the sanction of God for centuries, was, to the Jew as such, an insuperable difficulty.

Many Christians can hardly appreciate this difficulty, inasmuch as the truth of the Church is largely obscured in their minds, or even totally lost. Viewing the Church as the aggregate of all believers through all time, they have no difficulty in finding what they believe to be the Church in the Old Testament. That this has been the thought of godly men is amply proved by the headings they have given to many Old Testament chapters in the Authorized Version. Accept, however, the truth of the Church, as unfolded in the Epistle to the Ephesians, and at once we are faced with this difficulty which can only be met by the fact that the truth of *the Church is an entirely fresh revelation.*

This great truth which Paul had received by revelation he speaks of as "the mystery" and again in verse four as "the mystery of the Christ". In using the term mystery, Paul does not wish to convey the thought of anything mysterious—a purely human use of the word. In Scripture a mystery is something which has hitherto been kept secret, that could not be otherwise known than by revelation, and, when revealed, can only be apprehended by faith. The Apostle proceeds to explain that this mystery was not made known to the sons of men in the Old Testament days but *now* is made known by revelation unto the "holy apostles and prophets by the Spirit". The prophets spoken of are clearly not Old Testament prophets, any more than in chapter 2:20. In both cases the order is "apostles and prophets", not "prophets and apostles", as might be expected had the reference been to the prophets of the Old Testament. Moreover, the Apostle is speaking of what is "now" revealed, in contrast to what was formerly revealed.

What then is this mystery? It is clearly not the Gospel, which was not hidden in other ages. The Old Testament is full of allusions to the grace of God, and the coming Saviour, though these revelations were but little understood. We are plainly told in verse 6 that this new revelation is that the Gentiles "should be joint heirs, and a joint body and joint partakers of [His] promise in Christ Jesus by the glad tidings" (N.Tr.). The Gentiles are made joint heirs with the Jews, not in Christ's earthly kingdom, but in that far greater inheritance described in chapter 1 which includes both things in heaven and things on earth. And more, the Gentile believers are formed with Jewish believers into a joint body, of which Christ is the Head in heaven. Moreover they jointly partake of God's promise in Christ Jesus. The Gentile is not raised to the Jewish level on earth, nor is the Jew brought down to the Gentile level. Both are taken off their old standing and raised to an immeasurably higher plane, united to one another on entirely new and heavenly ground *in Christ*. And all this is brought to pass by the Gospel which addresses both on one common level of guilt and utter ruin. The three great facts referred to in this verse are unfolded in chapter 1. The promise in Christ includes all the blessings unfolded in the first seven verses of that chapter; the inheritance is opened out before us in verses 8-21, and the "one body" in verses 22 and 23.

The mystery can be thus briefly stated within the compass of a single verse, but to lay hold of the greatness of the truth and all that is involved therein, demands the deepest spiritual exercise. One has said, "It is wonderful how slow Christians are to understand the largeness of the counsels of God. ... In general we are obliged to be much more occupied with the details of the Christian life than with the great principles of this life." In the contemplation of the mystery we are carried back before the foundation of the world to find its source in the heart of the Father. There all was counselled according to His good pleasure. There too, in God, this great mystery remained hidden throughout the ages of time, until, in the ways of God, the moment was ripe for its revelation. Before that moment is reached great events must transpire: the world must be tested and proved to be an utterly ruined world: Christ must be manifested in the flesh and His redemption work accomplished: He must be raised from the dead and seated in the glory: lastly, the Holy Spirit must come to earth.

The presence of Christ on earth was the final and greatest test for man. Dwelling among men, full of grace and truth, He "went about doing good". On every hand He manifested a power that could relieve man of every possible ill—whether from sin, disease, death, or the devil. Moreover, with a heart filled with compassion, He manifested a grace that used His power on behalf of sinful men. In result, all this manifestation of divine goodness only brought to light the absolute hatred of man for the perfect goodness of God. It was the final demonstration of the complete ruin of man whether Jew or Gentile. The Jews utterly rejecting the long-promised Messiah, sealed their doom in saying, "We have no King but Cæsar." This was apostasy. The Gentiles proved their utter ruin by using the government that God had put into their hands to condemn the Son of God after having judicially pronounced Him innocent. The Cross was man's answer to God's love—the final proof that not only is man a sinner, but a ruined sinner, beyond all hope of recovery in himself. What happens? The Christ, that the world has rejected, ascends to glory, and the world comes under judgment. The light of the world is put out, and the world is left in darkness. The Prince of life is slain and the world is left in death. Death and darkness cover the whole scene, Jew and Gentile both alike, dead to God in trespasses and sins.

Is there, then no more hope for a ruined world? Must the world roll on to judgment with its vast freight of ruined souls? Has man been vanquished by sin and death? Has the Devil thwarted the purposes of God, encompassed man in hopeless ruin and triumphed over all? As far as man is concerned there is but one answer. All is ruined—irretrievably ruined. The Cross proves that it is not a *dying* world, but a *dead* world, "Because we thus judge, that if one died for all, then were all dead." But in this supreme crisis, when the end of the world is reached and its awful history of sin is closed in death, then God falls back upon His eternal counsels, acts according to His own good pleasure, and in due time discloses the secrets of His heart. If the world is dead, God lives, and the living God acts according to His counsels. The world had put the Christ of God upon a Cross of shame: God raises Christ from among the dead and seats Him upon a throne of glory; in due time, on the great day of Pentecost, the Spirit of God comes into the world from the glorified Christ. Wonderful indeed was that moment when the earth was waste and empty and darkness was upon the face of the deep and the Spirit of God moved upon the face of the waters; but far more wonderful the day when the Spirit of God came into a world that had ruined itself by putting out the light of the world and putting to death the Prince of life. May we not say that once again "darkness was upon the face of the deep", and once again "the Spirit of God moved upon the face of the waters"? God commences a new creation work based, not upon a dying man, but upon "Christ the Son of the living God"—the beginning of the Creation of God.

From the midst of a world of apostate Jews and godless Gentiles, God calls out a great company of quickened souls, redeemed by blood, and forgiven according to the riches of His grace; and not only calls them out of a ruined world but unites them in one body with Christ their Head in heaven. They are not of the world from which Christ has been rejected, even as He is not of the world (John 17:16), but they belong to heaven where Christ is seated, their risen and exalted Head. Moreover they will be associated with Christ in His glorious inheritance when He will have dominion over the whole created universe of God, whether they be things in heaven or things on earth.

Such then is this great mystery, in other ages not made known unto the sons of men, but now revealed unto His holy apostles and prophets by the Spirit, and ministered to us through the Apostle Paul. For of this great truth, as the Apostle tells us, he was made a minister (verse 7). It is not that it was not revealed to the other Apostles—Paul tells us that it was—but to him was committed the special service of ministering this truth to the saints. Hence only in the Epistles of Paul do we find any unfolding of the mystery. The *grace of God* had given this ministry to the apostle, and the *power of God* enabled him to exercise the gift of grace. God's gifts can only be used in God's power.

Moreover the Apostle tells us the effect this great truth had upon himself (verse 8). In the presence of the greatness of God's grace he sees that he is the chief of sinners (1 Timothy 1:15); in the presence of the immense vista of blessing unfolded by the mystery he feels that he is less than the least of all saints. The greater the glories that are opened to our vision the smaller we become in our own eyes. The man who had the largest apprehension of this great mystery in all its vast extent, was the man who owns he is less than the least of all saints.

In order to fulfil his ministry, the Apostle preached among the Gentiles the unsearchable riches of Christ (verse 8). Paul not only proclaimed the irretrievable ruin of man, but the unsearchable riches of Christ, riches beyond all human computation carrying blessings that have no limit. Could we search to the end of His riches we should not reach the limit of the blessings that these riches bestow.

The preaching of the Gospel, however, was in view of the second part of Paul's service, to enlighten all with the knowledge of "the administration of the mystery" (verse 9, N.Tr.). Not simply to enlighten all with the truth of the mystery but with the knowledge of how it is administered, to show all men how the counsel of God from eternity to eternity is brought about in time by the formation of the Assembly on earth, and thus bring to light in public that which has hitherto been hidden in God from the beginning of the world.

But more, not only would God have all men enlightened as to the formation of the Assembly on earth, but it is His intent that now all the heavenly beings should learn in the Church the manifold wisdom of God. These heavenly beings had seen the creation come fresh from the hands of God, and, as they beheld His wisdom in creation, they sang for joy. Now in the formation of the Church they see "the *all-various wisdom* of God" (verse 10, N.Tr.). Creation was the most perfect expression of creatorial wisdom; but in the formation of the Church God's wisdom is displayed in every form. Ere the Church could be formed God's glory had to be vindicated, man's need must be met, sin must be put away, death abolished, and the power of Satan annulled. The barrier must be removed between Jew and Gentile, heaven opened, Christ seated as a Man in the glory, the Holy Spirit come to earth and the Gospel preached. All this and more is involved in the formation of the Church, and these varied ends could be attained only by the all-various wisdom of God. Wisdom displayed, not only in one direction but in every direction. Thus the Church on earth becomes the lesson book of heavenly and angelic beings. Nor has the failure of the Church in its responsibilities, altered the fact that in the Church the angels learn this lesson. On the contrary, it only makes more manifest the marvellous wisdom that, rising above all man's failure, overcoming every obstacle, at last brings the Church to glory "according to the eternal purpose which He purposed in Christ Jesus our Lord."

In the following verses (12 and 13) the Apostle turns aside from the unfolding of the mystery to give a brief word as to its practical effect. These wonders are not unrolled before our vision simply to be admired, admirable indeed as they are, for as David said of the House of God, it is "exceeding magnifical". But it is equally true that the mystery is exceedingly practical, and in these two verses we see the effect of the mystery when rightly apprehended and acted upon. It is a truth that will make us at home in God's world, but put us outside man's world. As the blind man of John 9, when cast out by the religious world, finds himself in the presence of the Son of God, so Paul has access to the palace in heaven (verse 12), but finds himself in a prison on earth (verse 13). Christ Jesus, the One through whom all these eternal purposes will be fulfilled, is the One by whom we have access by faith to the Father. If in Christ we are going to be set before God holy, without blame, in love, then in Christ we have holy boldness even now, and access to the Father with confidence. This great truth makes us at home in the presence of the Father. But in the world it will lead to tribulation. This Paul found, but he says, "Faint not at my tribulations." To accept the truth of the mystery—to walk in the light of it, will at once put us outside the course of this world, and, above all, outside the religious world. Act upon this truth and at once we shall meet the opposition of the religious world. It will be with us as it was with Paul, a continual struggle, and especially with all that judaizes.

And it must be so, for these great truths entirely undermine the worldly constitution of every man-made religious system. Is the truth of the mystery, with the knowledge of which Paul sought to enlighten all men, proclaimed from the pulpits of Christendom, holiness conventions, or even from evangelical platforms? Is the truth of the mystery involving the total ruin of man, the utter rejection of Christ by the world, the session of Christ in glory, and the presence of the Holy Spirit on earth, the separation of the believer from the world and the calling of the saints to heaven—is this great truth proclaimed or acted upon in the national churches and religious denominations of Christendom? Alas! it has no place in their creeds, their prayers, or their teaching. Nay, more and worse, it is denied by their very constitution, their teaching and their practice.

But if this is so, we have a resource. We can pray, and hence these two verses (12 and 13) lead quite naturally to the prayer of the Apostle with which the chapter closes. If we have boldness and access with confidence, then *we can pray*. If we are faced with tribulations, then *we must pray*. So that in the presence of the special service given to Paul to minister the truth, and the tribulation in which this service involved him, he has only one resource, to bow his knees unto the Father of our Lord Jesus Christ.

The prayer in the first of Ephesians was addressed to the "God of our Lord Jesus Christ". There Christ is viewed as a Man in relation to God, and from Christ set over all we look down upon the inheritance spread out in all its vast extent of glory. Here the prayer is addressed to the "Father of our Lord Jesus Christ", and Christ is viewed as the Son in relation to the Father, and instead of looking down upon the inheritance we look up to divine Persons.

The request in the first prayer is that we might know the hope of His calling, the glory of His inheritance, and the exceeding greatness of His power. But this prayer rises beyond the calling, extends beyond the inheritance, and leads to that which is greater than power. For here the Apostle prays, not only that we may know the hope of the calling, but that Christ—the One in whom we are called—may dwell in our hearts; not only that we may know the riches of His inheritance, but that we may know the fulness of God; not only that we may know His exceeding power, but that we may know the love of Christ that passeth knowing.

In order that these requests may be granted, the Apostle prays that there might be a special work by the Holy Spirit in the inner man. In the first prayer the power is toward us, here the power worketh in us. There it was the enlightenment of the eyes to see the inheritance, here it is a work in the heart to comprehend the love. To enter into the deep things of God we must be rooted and grounded in love. To be rooted and grounded in the knowledge of the schools will be of no avail in learning the mysteries of God. Here we touch a region beyond the wit of man. We are in contact with things that eye hath not seen, nor ear heard, neither have entered into the heart of man, things which God alone can teach through our affections. Thus when Christ dwells in the heart by faith, and we are rooted and grounded in love, then we shall be able to comprehend with all saints what is the breadth and length, and depth and height. The Apostle does not exactly say to what these terms refer, but has he not in view the infinite counsels of God, long hidden, but now at last disclosed in the mystery? This it is possible to comprehend, but there is that which passeth knowing—the love of Christ. It can be perfectly enjoyed, but we shall never reach its end or fathom its depths.

Here we are launched upon a shoreless sea whose depths no line has ever fathomed. In the knowledge of this love we shall be filled with all the fulness of God. The "fulness of God" is that with which God is filled. Christ is the fulness of God, as we read, "in Him dwells all the fulness of the Godhead bodily" (Colossians 2:9, N.Tr.). The Church is the fulness of Christ—"the fulness of Him that filleth all in all" (Ephesians 1:23). God alone can lead our hearts into the knowledge of Christ's love and thus fill us with His fulness. For He is able to do exceedingly abundantly above all that we ask or think, according to the power that worketh in us. It is not doing things *for us*, however true that may be, but here it is doing a work *in us*. The Apostle is not speaking of our circumstances and daily needs, and all that His mercy can do for us; he is speaking of that vast universe of blessing into which He can lead our souls by a work in us. Nor does the Apostle say, "Above all that we *can* ask or think", as the verse is sometimes wrongly quoted. One has said, "There is a great difference between what we do ask and think, and what we *can* ask and think. There is no limit to what we may ask." Nor can we limit what God can do in the saints for their blessing and His glory.

This leads the Apostle to close with a burst of praise: "Unto Him be glory in the Church in Christ Jesus unto all generations of the age of ages. Amen" (N.Tr.). It was Paul's high privilege to administer the mystery in time, but, says Paul, let it be to the glory of God throughout eternity. Counselled in eternity before the foundation of the world it will exist for the glory of God throughout eternity, when the world shall be no more.

6.
The Church as the House of God According to the Mind of God

There are two main aspects in which the Church is viewed in the New Testament; one as the body of Christ, the other as the house of God.

When the Church is viewed in the former aspect, it is composed of all believers on earth formed into one body and united to one Head in heaven by the baptism of the Holy Spirit (1 Corinthians 12:12-13; Colossians 1:18). Viewing the Church as the house of God according to the mind of God, it is composed of Jewish and Gentile believers builded together for an habitation of God through the Spirit (Ephesians 2:22).

The one body presents the heavenly aspect of the Church. Believers are constituted a heavenly people by reason of their union with Christ in heaven as the Head of the body. The house of God, on the other hand, always presents the Church in connection with the earth.

The formation and maintenance of the one body is outside the responsibility of man, and hence nothing that is unreal has any part in the one body. It is true all believers are responsible to maintain the truth of the one body, and walk according to the light of it, and in this we have grievously failed; but the one body itself is formed only of true believers and by the Holy Spirit. The house of God, on the other hand, has been placed in the responsibility of man and, as ever, man breaks down; hence worthless material has been brought into the house of God leading to the solemn statement of the Apostle Peter that "Judgment must begin at the house of God" (1 Peter 4:17).

Before, however, we can form any just idea of our responsibilities in connection with the house of God, or estimate the extent of our failure in carrying out these responsibilities, it is essential to have clearly before our minds the house of God according to the original purpose of God. For this we must turn to the Word of God. It is impossible to learn from a corrupted Christendom the original purpose of the Divine Architect in having a house on earth.

Turning to Scripture, we are at once faced with the fact that the house of God has a very large place both in the Old Testament and the New. The first mention of it is in Genesis 28, the last in Revelation 21. From the first book to the last, from the present creation in time right on to the new heaven and new earth in eternity, the house of God is one of the great unchanging objects before the mind of God.

It is true the composition of the house is very different at different times. In the Old Testament days it was formed of boards and curtains, and later of material stones. Today, in the purpose of God, the house is composed of "living stones". But while its composition varies, the purpose of the house remains the same. Whatever form it takes, the purpose is ever to constitute a dwelling-place for God. Solomon expresses this thought when he says, "I have built an house of habitation for Thee and a place for Thy dwelling for ever" (2 Chronicles 6:2). God, for the gratification of His own heart, is determined to dwell with men.

It must, however, be evident that God's house must have certain characteristics. Whatever form it may take it must of necessity be suited to God. The first Epistle to Timothy was specially written to instruct us in the behaviour suited to the house of God (1 Timothy 3:15). But in order to [exhibit] right behaviour it is essential that we know the characteristic marks of God's house.

Holiness is the first great characteristic feature, as we read in Psalm 93:5, "Holiness becometh Thine house, O LORD, for ever." Again we read, in Ezekiel 43:12, "This is the law of the house; upon the top of the mountain the whole limit thereof round about shall be most *holy*. Behold, this is the law of the house." Holiness, then, is the first law of the house. In accord with this, Timothy is to charge those who form the house of God to maintain "love out of a pure heart, a good conscience and faith unfeigned", and moreover, to refuse all conduct contrary to sound teaching (1 Timothy 1:5-10). Furthermore, the house of God must be marked by *dependence upon God*, hence prayer has a large place in it, for prayer is the expression of dependence upon God. So we read, "I will therefore that men pray everywhere, lifting up holy hands" (1 Timothy 2:8). All that are in God's house must be dependent upon the God that dwells there. Moreover, another great characteristic is *subjection to authority*. In the house of God the woman is to learn in subjection and not usurp authority over the man (1 Timothy 2:11-12).

Finally, it is marked by *oversight* and *care*. Oversight in regard to the spiritual welfare of souls (1 Timothy 3:1-7), and care as to the temporal needs of the bodies of men (1 Timothy 3:8-13).

The world is marked by unholiness, independence, the revolt against all authority, with no spiritual oversight, and no adequate care for the bodies of men; but in the house of God entirely opposite conditions are to prevail. There according to the mind of God holiness must be maintained; there all must be in dependence upon God; there all must be in subjection to the authority that God has ordained; and there souls are fed, and bodies are cared for.

These, then, are some of the leading characteristics. Holiness, dependence, subjection, oversight, and care. Moreover, these characteristics are necessary in view of the purpose of God in His house being duly carried out.

What, then, is the great purpose that God has at heart in dwelling amongst men? First, if God has a dwelling-place among men it is in order that God may be known in blessing to men. Second, if man is blessed it is in order that God may be praised. These are the two great ends purposed in connection with the house of God. God made known to man in blessing in order that man may turn to God in praise.

In view of the purpose of God it becomes quite plain that the privilege and responsibility of those who have part in the house of God are to express God and to praise God. These leading principles are very beautifully presented in the first passage in Scripture that speaks of the house of God—Genesis 28:10-22. There Jacob, the houseless wanderer, has a vision of the house of God, and at once there passes before us the purpose of God and the responsibility of man in connection with God's house. God reveals Himself to Jacob as the One who is set upon blessing man in sovereign grace. "In thee," says God, "and in thy seed shall all the families of the earth be blessed." Moreover, what God has promised He will perform. He will be faithful to His own word. "I will not leave thee until I have done that which I have spoken to thee of." Then on our side we have the two-fold responsibility of man. Jacob says, "This is none other but the house of God and this is the gate of heaven." Thereupon he sets up "a pillar, and poured oil upon the top of it". The gate presents the thought of access to heaven. Through the gate we are enabled to get in touch with heaven for praise and prayer. And be it said this gate is not in some far-off place beyond the bounds of earth. The gate of heaven is always on earth, and here, while we are on earth, we are to use the gate. The pillar, as we know from the story of Jacob's parting with Laban, carries with it the thought of witness (Genesis 31:52). Thus we have our two-fold responsibility in connection with the house. On the one hand to approach God in prayer and praise, on the other to approach man as a witness for God—a witness that can only be carried out in the power of the Spirit, as set forth in the pillar with the oil poured out on the top.

Turning to 2 Chronicles 6 we shall see the purpose of God and the responsibility of man again presented at the dedication of the house built by king Solomon. First we see it is the place where God presents Himself in blessing to man. The king, representing the attitude of God to man, "turned his face, and blessed the whole congregation of Israel" (verse 3). Moreover, the king bears testimony to the faithfulness of God to His word, "The Lord, therefore, hath performed His word that He hath spoken (verses 4, 10, 15). Then on the side of man's responsibility and privilege we see that Solomon's temple becomes the gate of heaven. Nine times the king requests that prayer towards this place may be heard in heaven. The house becomes the gate of access to heaven (verses 21-40). Finally, the house that Solomon built was, like Jacob's pillar, to be a witness to God among all the nations of the earth, as he says, "That all people of the earth may *know* Thy Name, and fear Thee, as doth Thy people Israel, and may *know* that this house, which I have built, is called by Thy Name" (verse 33).

Turning to the New Testament, we see in the First Epistle of Peter that, though the form of the house of God has altered, the purpose of God, and the responsibilities of man, in connection with the house, remain the same. Here it is no longer a material house of dead stones, but a spiritual house of living stones. "Ye", says the apostle, "as living stones are built up a spiritual house" (1 Peter 2:5). In the first chapter of the Epistle we learn that those who form this house are the subjects of God's sovereign blessing, as we read, "Blessed be the God and Father of our Lord Jesus Christ, which according to His abundant mercy hath begotten us again unto a living hope by the resurrection of Jesus Christ from the dead, to an inheritance incorruptible and undefiled and that fadeth not away, reserved in the heavens (N.Tr.) for you." Then we further learn that this blessing is secured by "The Word of the Lord", which "endureth for ever."

Passing on to chapter 2 we find the presentation of our privileges and responsibilities in connection with the house. On the one hand we are built together "to offer up spiritual sacrifices acceptable to God by Jesus Christ." On the other, before men, we are to "shew forth the excellencies of Him (N.Tr.) who hath called us out of darkness into His marvellous light." Here, then, we have once again "the gate of heaven" and "the pillar" with the anointing oil. We draw nigh to God to offer up praise and prayer, we draw nigh to men as a witness of His excellencies.

Finally we may ask when did the house of God, in its present form, come into existence? Very definitely Scripture answers—Not until redemption was accomplished. If God is to come into the midst of a praising people, then Christ must first go into the darkness and forsaking of the cross. There we hear that cry, "My God, My God, why hast Thou forsaken Me?" And the One that uttered the cry alone can give the answer, "Thou art holy, O Thou that *inhabitest the praises of Israel*." If the holy God is to dwell in the midst of a praising people, Christ must redeem a people by going into death.

Jacob, as we have seen, may speak of the house of God, but not until redemption is accomplished does God speak of dwelling among the children of Israel (*see* Exodus 29:45). Neither with Adam the innocent nor with Abraham the faithful could God dwell. He may indeed walk in the garden, and grant a passing visit to Abraham, but neither innocence nor faithfulness secured a dwelling-place for God. Mere innocence would not suit God's house; the faithfulness of man would not secure it when innocence was lost. God's dwelling amongst men is the fruit of redemption, for therein is the believer made fit for God, and therein is a holy God made known to man. It is clear that "the house of God which is the Assembly of the living God" had no existence until redemption was accomplished. Then on the day of Pentecost, the disciples being together in one place at Jerusalem, the Holy Spirit descended and "filled all the house where they were sitting", and "they were all filled with the Holy Spirit". The people of God who had hitherto been scattered abroad were then formed into the habitation for God, and God took up His dwelling-place in the house.

7.
The Church as the House of God in the Hands of Men

In the last chapter we sought to learn from Scripture the truth of the house of God when viewed according to the mind of God. We have seen the purpose of God in dwelling amongst men, and the responsibilities of men in connection with God's dwelling .

We have now to inquire, has man answered to his responsibilities? Alas! the history of the ages has proved that man in responsibility has invariably broken down; the higher the privilege and the greater the responsibility, the greater the breakdown. Hence in nothing has the failure of man been so complete as in connection with the Church viewed as the house of God on earth.

To form a true estimate of the extent of this failure it is essential to obtain a clear view of the house of God according to God's original plan. In the days when the children of Israel were in captivity, because of their failure to maintain the holiness of God's house, the prophet Ezekiel is told *to "shew the house* to the house of Israel, that they may be ashamed of their iniquities; and let them measure the pattern" (Ezekiel 43:10). Only thus would it be brought home to them how great had been their departure from the pattern.

As we have seen in the history of Jacob, man's responsibility in connection with the house was set forth by "the gate" and "the pillar". The gate of heaven being Godward and expressing our privilege and responsibility to draw nigh to God in prayer and praise; the pillar, with the oil, being manward and setting forth our responsibility to maintain a true witness for God before men. We have failed in both directions, we have not adequately used the gate of Heaven, and consequently we have not reared our pillar. We have failed in prayer and dependence upon God, and therefore we have failed in testimony before men.

Moreover, it must be admitted that, in order that the house of God may be a true expression of God, there must be the maintenance of the characteristic marks of the house. For all the characteristics of God's house have in view the true expression of God Himself. Hence in the house holiness must be maintained in order that there may be a true expression of God. Then, too, prayer is to be made for "all men", because this expresses God's desire that all men should be saved. Women are to be marked by modesty and "good works", for in good works there is the setting forth of the goodness of God to man. So, too, the house is to be marked by the care of souls and bodies, for thus it will be seen that God has at heart the welfare of men.

Finally the house of God is to be marked by "godliness" (1 Timothy 3:14-16). It is obvious that none other than godly behaviour is suited to the house of God. Seeing that the great purpose of God's house is to express God, it will become plain that godliness consists in a life that makes God manifest. Hence it is not sanctimoniousness, nor is it merely an amiable and benevolent life such as it is possible for the natural man to exhibit. The godly life is a life lived in the fear of God and hence *the life that expresses God*. The secret of this life lies in having before our souls the perfect pattern of godliness as set forth in Christ. Thus in the closing verses of the third chapter of 1st Timothy, the apostle gives a remarkable summary of the life of Christ, from the incarnation to the ascension, in which the Spirit of God has brought together certain great facts in that life which express God. God *manifest* in the flesh, *seen* of angels, *preached* unto the Gentiles, believed on in the world, received up into glory, are all facts that make the heart of God known to man. Thus we learn in Christ the secret of godliness or the life that expresses God.

What a marvellous expression of God there would have been in the sight of the world if the Church as the house of the living God had remained true to the principles of God's house. The world would have seen a company of people marked by holiness, dependence upon God, subjection to authority, good works, and care for bodies and souls. They would have seen the setting forth of principles entirely opposite to those which prevail in the fallen world, and above all, they would have learnt the attitude of God towards man. Alas! it is evident from every point of view that those who compose the house of God have utterly failed. We have failed to maintain the great principles of God's house and thus have failed to give a true expression of God before the world.

How has this failure been brought about? The history of Israel, and their failure in connection with the house of God in their day, may disclose to us the secret of our own failure. The prophet Ezekiel is told to say to the "rebel-

THE CHURCH AS THE HOUSE OF GOD IN THE HANDS OF MEN

lious" house of Israel, "Ye have brought into My sanctuary strangers, uncircumcised in heart, and uncircumcised in flesh, to be in My sanctuary, to pollute it, even My house, … and ye have not kept the charge of Mine holy things: but ye have set keepers of My charge in My sanctuary for yourselves" (Ezekiel 44:6-8). Here we have three definite charges; they introduced into the house those who had no part nor lot in the house; they failed to maintain the holiness of the house; and they used the house of God for their own ends—"for themselves".

Has this not been the sad history of the house of God in the present dispensation? On the day of Pentecost those who formed the house of God by the descent of the Holy Spirit were no "strangers", all were true children of God. There were no "uncircumcised in heart" among the three thousand added to the Church by the Lord. Every one was a true believer. But alas! how soon the "stranger" was brought in. By the baptism of Simon Magus one was introduced into the company where the Spirit of God dwelt, who had no part nor lot in the matter; others soon followed, with the result that even in the apostles' day the house of God became likened to a great house in which "there are not only vessels of gold and of silver, but also of wood and of earth; and some to honour, and some to dishonour" (2 Timothy 2:20). Thus, as with Israel of old, the holiness of the house has not been maintained and men are using the house of God for their own ends, "teaching things which they ought not, for the sake of base gain" (Titus 1:11, N.Tr.). The evils of the apostles' days have been increasing through the ages, until, in these last days, there is a vast mass of lifeless profession in the house of God marked by the form of godliness without the power (2 Timothy 3:1-5).

What, then, is the result of the failure of man in responsibility? As in Israel's case, the evil that as been brought into the house of God calls aloud for judgment. "The time is come that judgment must begin at the house of God" (1 Peter 4:17).

In Israel's day the time came when the Lord refused to recognize the temple as the house of God. He had to say, "Behold, *your house* is left unto you desolate" (Matthew 23:38). All the true children of God in connection with the temple were added to the Church, and the desolate house passed on to judgment. Again, the Church as the house of God has become corrupted, and very soon all that is of God will be caught away to meet the Lord in the air, and the vast mass of godless profession, no longer owned as the house of God, will pass on to judgment.

Has, then, God's purpose to dwell amongst men been thwarted by the failure of man in responsibility? Surely not. No lapse of time, no change of dispensation, no failure of God's people, no opposition of the enemy, no power of death, can for one moment move the heart of God from His determined purpose to have His house on earth and dwell among men.

The moment a redeemed people are secured, God discloses the desire of His heart to dwell in their midst (*see* Exodus 15:13, 17; 29:45). The tabernacle in the wilderness, and the temple in the land, bear their witness to God's cherished thought. And though the people fail and neglect the house, though their temple is destroyed, and they pass into captivity, yet not for one moment will God surrender His purpose to dwell in the midst of His people. He brings back a remnant to rebuild His house; they, too, utterly fail and in their turn are scattered among the nations, and once again the house is left without a stone

THE CHURCH AS THE HOUSE OF GOD IN THE HANDS OF MEN

upon a stone. Nevertheless, God pursues His glorious way. Rising above all the failure of men, He discloses fresh secrets of His heart and brings to light "the house of God which is the assembly of the living God, the pillar and base of the truth." But again man in responsibility breaks down, the house of God becomes a ruin; instead of being marked by holiness it is likened to the great house of a mere man in which there are vessels to honour and dishonour. A little remnant may indeed separate from the vessels to dishonour and seek to return to the moral features of the house of God and walk according to the principles which govern the house of God, but they, too, break down, and the responsibility of man closes in judgment that commences at the house of God. Nevertheless, though all breaks down in the hands of men, whether it be Israel of old or the Church in the present day, yet God remains true to His purpose, and there rises up before us the vision of another house, in a millennial day, and "the latter glory of this house shall be greater than the former".

Yet even so this house will pass away, for the glorious millennial age will end in gloom and judgment. But God will not give up His purpose, for beyond the judgment of the nations, and beyond the judgment of the great white throne, there is unrolled before us "a new heaven and a new earth" and, in that fair scene, we see "the holy city new Jerusalem, coming down from God out of heaven, prepared as a bride adorned for her husband", and we hear "a great voice out of Heaven saying, *Behold, the tabernacle of God is with men, and He will dwell with them*, and they shall be His people, and God Himself shall be with them and be their God." We have travelled beyond the bounds of time with all its changes and its broken responsibilities. We have reached eternity with its new heaven and new earth; we have passed into a scene where all tears are wiped away, where "there shall be no more death, neither sorrow nor crying, neither shall there be any more pain; for the former things are passed away". And there we see God's great purpose throughout the ages at last fulfilled, never more to be marred by the power of the enemy or the failure of the saints.

8.
The Church as the Body of Christ

In former chapters, after taking a general view of the truth concerning the Church, we considered a special aspect of it—the house of God. There is, however, another important aspect in which the Church is presented in Scripture, namely as the body of Christ. This we may briefly consider.

In reference to this aspect of the Church, the language of Scripture is very precise. We read in Colossians 1:18, that Christ "is the Head of the body, the Church", and again in 1 Corinthians 12:12-13, that "as the body is one, and hath many members, and all the members of that one body, being many, are one body, so also is Christ. For by one Spirit are we all baptized into one body, whether we be Jews or Gentiles, whether we be bond or free; and have been all made to drink into one Spirit." From these Scriptures it is plain that all believers are formed into one body by the Holy Spirit on earth with one Head in heaven. We have seen that men were introduced by baptism with water into the Christian profession which forms the house of God on earth. It is clear, however, that no baptism by water can bring people into the body of Christ. This can only be effected by the baptism of the Holy Spirit. Hence nothing but what is real can have any part in the body of Christ. In thinking of the body of Christ we must look at Christians solely in the light of God's work in them. It is true the flesh is yet in us, but God has condemned it, and viewing us apart from it, sees us "in Christ" and "in the Spirit". That is, God ever views His people in connection with Christ and the Spirit, and we are privileged to view ourselves in the same way. Another has said, "It is in this light only that we can speak of the membership of the body; nothing finds place in any way in the body of Christ but what is of Christ—of God. There is no such thing imaginable in the body of Christ as failure or flesh." Those who compose the body, having the flesh in them, may indeed fail to walk in correspondence to the truth, but in the body itself all is of Christ. It is His body.

There are three portions of Scripture which, in a special way, present this great truth: Ephesians 1 and 2; Colossians 1 and 3; and 1 Corinthians 12 and 14. In Ephesians the body is presented in its eternal aspect according to the counsels of the Father. In Colossians it is viewed in its time aspect as the vessel for the display of Christ. In Corinthians the body is introduced as the instrument for the manifestations of the Spirit on earth.

The manifestations of the Spirit through the body have in view the display of Christ in the body in time; and the display of Christ now is but the prelude to the setting forth of Christ in His fulness in the ages to come according to the counsels of the Father.

First, then, we may consider the truth of *the body according to the Father's counsels*. In Ephesians 1 the great subject

THE CHURCH AS THE BODY OF CHRIST

is the Father's purpose for the glory of Christ. The chapter unfolds "the mystery of His will according to His good pleasure which He purposed in Himself for the administration of the fulness of times; to head up all things in the Christ" (verses 9-10, N.Tr.). Moreover, in these counsels the Church has a place of highest privilege in connection with the glory of Christ, and hence we also learn the future destiny of the Church as the body of Christ. Here the Church is viewed, not in relation to present time, but in relation to the "fulness of times". We are permitted to look beyond the present moment, with all its failure, and see the future glory of the Church as the body of Christ. In that day "the Church which is His body" will be "the fulness of Him that filleth all in all" (verses 22-23). According to the counsel of God the day is coming when Christ will fill all things. The whole universe will be filled with blessing through Christ, but, in that day, it will be the special privilege of the Church to express "*the fulness of Him that filleth all in all.*" Though all will be blessed through Christ, and be to the glory of Christ, yet all will not express His fulness. This will be reserved for the Church. An individual saint may display some trait of Christ, all things in the world to come will display Christ in yet larger measure, but only in the Church as the body of Christ will there be the perfect display of Christ in all His fulness. Fulness gives the thought of completeness. Thus not only will Christ be displayed, but He will be displayed in perfection. That is, not only every excellence of Christ will be seen, but all will be seen in right proportion. No one trait will predominate, all will be displayed in perfect proportion and relation to one another, in the same way that the members of a normal human body are all in proportion and set forth the mind of the head. But what will be actually true then should be morally true now.

This leads to the truth of *the body as the vessel for the display of Christ in time*. For this aspect of the Church, as the body of Christ, we must turn to the Epistle to the Colossians. The great object of this epistle is to unfold the glories of Christ as the Head. We read in chapter 1:18, "He is the Head of the body the Church". It is, moreover, God's desire that the moral glories of the Head in heaven should have a present display in the body on earth. Hence the apostle, having spoken of the ministry of the Gospel, passes on to speak of a second ministry in connection with the body of Christ "which is the Church" (verse 24). He speaks of this truth as "the mystery which hath been hid from ages and from generations, but *now* is made manifest to His saints." Moreover, he speaks of the glory of this mystery as "*Christ in you*, the hope of glory".

The apostle lays special emphasis on these two great facts. First, the particular moment when the mystery is revealed, and second, the special glory of this mystery at the present time. These two great facts have a direct bearing on one another. Why, we may ask, is the mystery made known "now", and not before? Because three great events had come to pass without which the Church could not exist as a fact or be made known as a truth. Christ had been exalted as the glorious Head in heaven, the Holy Spirit had come to earth, and lastly, Christ had been finally rejected by the Jew.

The first two events were absolutely necessary before the Church could be formed. There must be the Head in heaven before there could be the body on earth, and the Holy Spirit must come to dwell in the members and thus form them into one body on earth with one Head in heaven. But the body existed as a fact before the truth was made known. For this the third great event was necessary. If the truth of Jew and Gentile being formed into one body, had been revealed before Christ was rejected, it would have contradicted all the express promises of God to the Jew under the first covenant. But when the Jew had finally rejected Christ the first covenant was definitely at an end, and the way is prepared for unfolding the truth of the Church as the body of Christ. The rejection was final and complete when Stephen was stoned. By the Cross man had rejected Christ on earth, and by the martyrdom of Stephen they rejected Christ in heaven. They stoned the man that witnessed to the fact that Christ is in heaven. Thus the moment arrived to disclose the great secret that though Christ Himself has been rejected, His body is on earth. Mark, not that sinners saved by grace will be in heaven—that is the Gospel and there is no mystery about it, the dying thief knew that—but the secret is now revealed that Christ has the Church—His body—in the place of His rejection during the time of His rejection. The first intimation of this great truth is given in connection with the conversion of the man who was made the minister of this truth. The Lord says to Saul, "Saul, Saul, why persecutest thou Me?" It is not, "Why do you persecute My disciples", or "those belonging to Me", or "those who are part of Me", but "Why persecutest thou ME?" As one has said, "In that little word is conveyed the fact that Christ is *here*."

Moreover, if Christ is here in those that form His body, it is that Christ may be displayed by His body. And Christ displayed in the Church now is "the hope of glory". In glory, as we have seen from the Epistle to the Ephesians, Christ will be displayed in His fulness. But the hope of glory is to have a present fulfilment. Hence the apostle passes on to show how Christ in the saints is to work out in the display of Christ by the saints. Thus God's present thought for the body—composed of all saints at any given moment on the earth—is that therein there should be the setting forth of Christ morally, and thus the body on earth correspond to the Head in heaven.

In the second chapter of Colossians the apostle shows how God has wrought to bring this to pass, and warns us of the different devices by which the devil seeks to frustrate the present purpose of God in the saints. First we are warned against the delusive opinions of men, presented in the most attractive way by persuasive speech (verse 4); then philosophy, or the love of human wisdom drawn from the traditions of men and the elements of the world (verse 8); further we are warned against religious flesh, connected with abstinence from certain food and the observance of certain days (verse 16); finally we are warned against superstition, such as worshipping angels (verse 18).

If we are to display the moral beauties of Christ we must know Christ. We must know the One whose character we are to set forth. The opinions of men, the philosophy of man, the religion of the flesh, and the superstitions of men will neither teach us anything of the character of Christ nor enable us to set forth that character when known.

Having warned us concerning the snares of the enemy we are instructed as to the provision that God has made in order that the moral perfections of the Head may be set forth in the body. In this connection four great truths are stated:

1st. We are "complete *in Him*" (verse 10).

2nd. We are identified *"with Him"* (verses 11, 13).

3rd. We are *of Him*: "the body is of Christ" (verse 17).

4th. We derive all spiritual nourishment *"from Him"* (verse 19).

THE CHURCH AS THE BODY OF CHRIST

1. *We are "complete in Him".* In Him there dwelleth all the fulness of the Godhead, therefore, everything that we can possibly need in order that we may know Christ and display Christ is found in Him—we are complete in Him. We are entirely independent of man as man. His opinions, his philosophy, and his religion cannot bring us to Christ, cannot unfold His character to us, or enable us to set forth His moral beauties.

2. *We are identified "with Him".* At the cross, in burial, in resurrection, and in life, God has identified the believer with Christ. At the cross—set forth by circumcision—Christ actually died to everything after the flesh; in burial He actually passed out of sight; in resurrection He actually passed forever out of the dominion of death, and as quickened He passed into a scene of glory in a life and condition that is wholly suited to the glory of God. Now what is actually true of Christ is true of the saints in the sight of God who identifies us "with Him", and faith sees with God. We know that our flesh has been put off in the death of Christ; and not only put off but put out of sight, for we are "buried with Him in baptism". Moreover, in spirit we are risen with Him, so that death has lost its power over us. And though our mortal bodies are not yet quickened, as to our souls, we live to God in that heavenly life set forth in Christ.

3. *We are of His order—"the body is of Christ".* The ordinances of the law were but shadows and were given to the first man who is of the earth earthly. But the things to come, of which the ordinances were but the shadow, are of Christ, the heavenly Man. And if Christ is heavenly, the body which is

of Christ is also heavenly. "As the heavenly One, such also the heavenly ones." For the moment we are on earth, but we are of the heavenly Man, and we thus belong to heaven.

4. *We derive all nourishment from the Head.* If the Church is heavenly it can only be nourished from heaven. There is nothing of earth that can minister to the man of heaven. There is nothing of man as such that can minister nourishment to the body, bind the members together, or lead to spiritual increase. All must come from the Head in heaven, ministered to the body through the joints and bands of the body. As the Head in heaven is for the nourishment of the body on earth, so the body on earth is for the display of the Head in heaven. Through not holding the Head, we may fail to set forth the Head, but Christ—the Head—will never fail to nourish His body; He cares for the body and every member of the body.

These four great facts—that we are "complete in Him", that we are identified "with Him", are of Him, and derive all nourishment from Him—all lead to the fulfilment of God's present purpose for the body, namely, the setting forth of the character of the Head in the body. This is seen in a practical way in the exhortations that follow.

Based on the doctrine of the Church in the first two chapters we are exhorted to "put on therefore, as the elect of God, holy and beloved, bowels of compassion, kindness, lowliness, meekness, long-suffering; forbearing one another, and forgiving one another, if any should have a complaint against any; even as the Christ has forgiven you, so also do ye. And to all these add love, which is the bond of perfectness. And let the peace of Christ preside in your hearts, to which also ye have been called in one body, and be ye thankful" ([Colossians] 3:12-15, N.Tr.). This is the lovely character of Christ, marked by *grace* with its unlimited forgiveness, by *love* binding all other perfections together, and by *peace* ruling the heart, which the saints, in the unity of "one body", are called to display while yet in the scene of Christ's absence and waiting for the day of His appearing.

What a beautiful setting forth of Christ there would be if the saints, as "one body", were marked by grace, and love, and peace. Though in a day of ruin our practice falls far short of this beautiful picture, let us not lower the standard. One has truly said, "Even if practice may not come up to it, and even if it is impossible to bring saints back to the real standard, let us have the right idea. It is a great thing to get the right idea; but then if we get it, let us expect that the Lord will give grace to walk according to the right idea, in the truth of it, even though you may not expect to see things restored to what they were when first established."

9.
The Church as the Body of Christ (continued)

1 CORINTHIANS 12

We have seen that the Church, as the body of Christ, is viewed in Scripture in a threefold way. First, in the Epistle to the Ephesians, in connection with the counsels of the Father; second, in the Epistle to the Colossians, as the vessel for the display of Christ; third, in 1 Corinthians 12, as the instrument for the manifestations of the Spirit.

In the last chapter we viewed the body in the first two aspects. It remains to briefly look at the body in connection with the manifestations of the Spirit brought before us in 1 Corinthians 12. The subject, however, of this chapter is not the body, but the Spirit. The body is introduced as the instrument which the Spirit uses for the display of Christ.

The ruin of Christendom has been largely brought about by the loss of all sense of the presence and power of the Holy Spirit. Clerisy, human organization, and the adoption of carnal methods, have set aside the Holy Spirit.

THE CHURCH AS THE BODY OF CHRIST (CONTINUED)

Hence the great importance of this chapter in which the rights of the Holy Spirit in the assembly are maintained, and instruction is given as to the true character of spiritual manifestations.

Taking a rapid view of the chapter we first notice in verses 2 and 3, *the aim of spiritual manifestations*. The great end that the Holy Spirit ever has in view, whatever form the manifestations take, is to exalt Christ. He ever leads to the confession of Jesus as Lord. Admitting this we are at once able to test the spirit by which men speak. It is not a question of distinguishing between a believer and an unbeliever, but of testing the spirit by which men speak. Is it by an evil spirit, or is it by the Spirit of God? If one is speaking by an evil spirit, however learned the speaker, however eloquent the discourse, however apparently moral the tone, in some form or other Christ will be degraded. If one is speaking by the Holy Spirit, however simple the discourse or unlearned the speaker, Christ will be exalted. Apply this test to Unitarians, to Higher Critics, or Modernists, and at once they are exposed, for, in different ways, all unite in robbing Christ of His glory.

But though all who speak by the Holy Spirit exalt Christ, it does not follow that all have the same gift. This leads the apostle in verses 4 to 6 to speak of *the diversity of spiritual gifts*. The apostle tells us there are diversities of gifts; at the same time we are reminded that diversity of gifts does not sacrifice unity of aim. For the diversity of gifts are controlled by the same Spirit, and thus all lead to the exaltation and expression of Christ (verse 4).

Moreover, the different gifts exercised by the Spirit have in view different forms of *service* under the control of one Lord who directs the service (verse 5).

Furthermore the exercise of the gifts in different services will produce different effects in *operations* on souls, but it is the same God who works all that is wrought in all (verse 6).

These verses (4-6) rebuke, and at the same time correct much of the grave disorder in Christendom. For the exercise of gift in Christendom, human ability, human wisdom, and a theological training is demanded as a preliminary necessity. No, says the apostle, you require that which no schools of men can give and no human attainments can supply—you require the power and energy of the Holy Spirit.

The religious world demands that you must be ordained of men, and have the authority of man before ministering to others. No, says the apostle, service according to God requires the authority and direction of the Lord, and will endure no rival authority.

Again we are apt to think that by eloquence and moving appeals an impression will be made on the souls of men. No, says the apostle, it is "God which worketh all in all." God worketh *everything* that is divine, in *everyone* in whom there is a vital work.

Having spoken of diversities of gifts the apostle, in verses 7 to 11, proceeds to speak of *the distribution of spiritual manifestations*. It is important to notice that it is not simply the gifts that are said to be given but the *manifestations* of the gifts. That is, the apostle is speaking primarily of the exercise of the gifts. Hence it is not simply "wisdom" but "*the word* of wisdom"; not only "knowledge" but "*the word* of knowledge"; not simply "miracles" but "*the working* of miracles". Four important truths are pressed. First, whatever the character of the manifestations and however

THE CHURCH AS THE BODY OF CHRIST (CONTINUED)

distributed, all flow from *the same Spirit* (verses 8-10). Thus unity is maintained.

Second, the Spirit distributes the manifestations of the gifts to *"every man"* (verses 7, 11). He entirely refuses to concentrate all His manifestations in "one man", or in a particular "class of men". This rebukes that greatest of all disorders in Christendom—the setting apart of a special class of men for the ministry and thus dividing the professing people of God into clergy and laity. Scripture allows of no such distinction. Christendom in its practice contradicts God's order and says the manifestations of the Spirit are given to "one man" who presides over the assembly. No, says the apostle, it is to "every man" in the assembly.

Third, the manifestation of the Spirit is given to every man *"to profit withal"*. It is given in view of the common good. It is not given for the exaltation or prominence of the individual, for obtaining personal influence or gain, or as a means of livelihood. It is given for profit—spiritual profit.

Fourth, the Spirit distributes the manifestation to every man severally *"as He will"* (verse 11). This shuts out the will of man. We must then leave room for the Spirit to work according to His will. If we appoint the minister or arrange the ministry, we shall be putting restrictions upon His will by the employment of our wills, and thus hinder the Holy Spirit's using whom He will.

Having spoken of the distribution of the gifts, and shown that the "working" of the gifts is by the Spirit, the apostle proceeds to speak, in verses 12 to 27 of *the instrument for spiritual manifestations*. This introduces the body of Christ. It is well to note that the body is only actually mentioned in verses 13 and 27. In all the other verses the apostle is speaking of the human body as an illustration. Apart from this great truth there can be no intelligent use of gift. For, according to God's order, the Spirit does not use us as isolated individuals, but as members of the body of Christ, and for the good of the whole body. Using the human body as an illustration, the apostle shows that as the human body is one, and yet composed of many members, each having a special place and function in the body, "so also is the Christ." This is a striking way of presenting the truth. The subject is the one body, but the apostle does not say, "so also is the body of Christ", but "so also is the Christ." Because the one body is viewed under the eye of God as the expression of Christ. This one body has been formed by the baptism of the Holy Spirit, and it has been truly said that the baptism of the Spirit was not intended to take us to heaven, but that there might be one body on earth which should be morally a reproduction of Christ. To enter into the true significance of the one body we must remember two facts. First, that Christ personally is absent from the world, second, that the Holy Spirit is present in the world; and during the time of Christ's absence Jewish and Gentile believers have been formed into one body, by the Holy Spirit, in order that Christ characteristically may be reproduced in His body—that all that He did in perfection in His body when here—pastoring, teaching, preaching and blessing—may be continued in His mystical body now that He is gone.

This baptism of the Holy Ghost took place in connection with Jewish believers at Pentecost (*see* Acts 1:5 and 2:1-4); and in reference to Gentile believers at the call of Cornelius and his friends (Acts 10:44, and 11:15-17). The baptism of the Spirit involves the setting aside of all that is after the flesh. Natural distinctions such as Jew or Gentile, and social positions such as bond or free, have no

THE CHURCH AS THE BODY OF CHRIST (CONTINUED)

place in the one body. We cannot think of ourselves as Jews or Gentiles, or according to any other fleshly distinction, for "by *one Spirit* are we all baptized into one body". All forming the one body have been "made to drink of one Spirit." We enjoy the same blessings and privileges, for this enjoyment springs from one source— the Holy Spirit.

From this point the apostle again takes up the human body to enforce certain practical truths in connection with spiritual manifestations in the one body. First, he presses that in the body there is *diversity in unity* (verses 14-19). "The body is not one member but many"; that is, while there is one body there are many members. But this diversity would be entirely lost, and the gravest disorder ensue if each member neglected its own function through envy of members having perhaps a higher function. If the foot began to complain because it was not a hand, and the ear complain that it was not an eye, the work of the body would cease, for complaining members cease to work effectually for the good of the body. How then is disorder prevented amongst the many members? By the recognition that it is God who hath "set the members every one of them in the body as it hath pleased Him." So in the body of Christ it is God that has given each his appointed place and function, with the result that *no member is pre-eminent*. The pre-eminence of one member would do away with the body altogether. "If they were all one member, where were the body?"

Furthermore the apostle presses the other side of the truth. There is *unity in diversity* (verses 20-24). If there are many members, we must remember there is only one body. But the unity of the body would be imperilled if the higher members were to look with disdain upon the lower. We have seen that envy of one another would break up the diversity, now we learn that disdain would break up the unity. If the eye treats the hand with contempt, and the head sneers at the feet, all unity of the body would be gone. What meets this danger? Again the recognition of God's own work. God hath tempered the body together in such fashion that no member can do without the other. The greatest member requires the least—nay, much more those members of the body which seem to be more feeble are necessary. It is not simply that all work to the common good, but that no one member can properly carry out its functions without the other members—in a word, *every member is indispensable.*

There are thus two grave dangers that can bring in disorder into the body. One, discontent on the part of the less prominent members with the place allotted to them; the other, disdain on the part of the more prominent members for those which seem to be more feeble. One breaks up the diversity, the other destroys the unity; both destroy the proper functions of the body. Bring God in, and in each case the disorder is met. It is God that has given each member his special work, and God has so tempered together the members of the body that *no member is preeminent and every member is indispensable.*

The result of God's work and wisdom is that the members of the human body have "the same care one for another" (verse 25). Not simply that they "take care of one another", but that they have a mutual interest in one another, so that if "one member suffer, all the members suffer with it; or one member be honoured, all the members rejoice with it." The apostle does not say that this should be so, but that it is so. In the application to the body of Christ the expression of this truth is greatly hindered by sectarianism, and denominational barriers that have been set up by man; but the truth remains that what affects one mem-

THE CHURCH AS THE BODY OF CHRIST (CONTINUED)

ber affects all members because the members are united to one another by the Holy Spirit, and what depends upon the Spirit abides, however much our failure may hinder its expression. The broken condition of the people of God has lowered our spiritual sensibilities; but the more we are controlled by the Spirit the deeper will be our realization of this truth. As one has said, "We consciously suffer or rejoice in the measure of our spiritual power."

The apostle has been speaking of the human body as the figure of the body of Christ. Now he gives these truths a local application. He says to the Corinthian saints, "Ye are body of Christ, and members in particular." He does not say, "Ye are *the* body of Christ", as the Authorized translation has it. The Corinthian assembly was not "the whole body of Christ", but they were the local expression of the one body. Such is the privilege and responsibility of the local assembly. They are "body of Christ", not independently—which would deny the truth of the one body, but representatively, which maintains the truth.

To-day we could hardly say of any local company of saints, "ye are body of Christ", for no local company includes all the saints in a given locality; and even did it do so, to assume to be the body of Christ in the place would be mere pretension. In the beginning, the local assembly represented what was visibly true of the whole. To-day, the Church is in ruin, and any company assuming to be the body of Christ is pretending to express something that is not true of the professing Church. It would be mere independency. Alas, as to fact, the various communities are locally only the expression of their respective denominations. However, it is still our responsibility to refuse to go on with anything that denies this great truth and our privilege and blessing to walk in the light of it.

10.
The Church in a Day of Ruin

2 Timothy 2

In a former chapter we sought to present the mind of God as to His house. We have also seen that, through the failure of man in responsibility, evil doctrines and evil men have been brought into the house of God, reducing the house to a ruin, and exposing it to judgment.

It has been pointed out that while the 1st Epistle to Timothy presents the house of God in order according to the mind of God, the 2nd Epistle presents the house when it has become ruined by the failure of man, and, in its ruin, likened to "a great house" in which "there are not only vessels of gold and of silver, but also of wood and of earth; and some to honour, and some to dishonour" (2 Timothy 2:20). The believer who has once seen the truth of the Assembly, as the house of God, as unfolded in Scripture, may well say, "I see nothing on earth that answers to the truth." Alas, this is true! In a day of ruin the truth of the house of God can only be known in an abstract way, there being no longer any concrete expression of the truth. All that can be actually seen in

THE CHURCH IN A DAY OF RUIN

Christendom is "a great house" containing vessels to honour and dishonour. This raises other questions in the mind of the believer, who desires to walk in obedience to God—Does the Word of God give any directions for God's people in a day of ruin? Is there any light as to how we are to walk, and with whom we are to walk, in a day when Christendom has become corrupt? However great the difficulties, or however dark the day, it is not possible to think that God ever leaves His people without sufficient light for their pathway through this world. Through lack of spirituality we may fail to discern the light; through lack of devotedness we may fail to walk according to the light, or through sheer apathy we may be wholly indifferent to it, nevertheless we may be sure the Word of God provides full light for our pathway.

There are three facts of the first importance for our souls to realize, if we desire to walk through this world according to the mind of God.

First, we have to learn that, however great our natural intelligence, however highly the mind may have been trained, however great our knowledge of Scripture, however sincere our desires, we cannot, if trusting to our own minds, find God's path for His people in the midst of the confusion of Christendom. We are not competent to find our way through the increasing difficulties of the path, to face the continual opposition to the truth, or to solve the various questions that constantly arise.

But, secondly, having discovered our utter incompetency it is a very great relief to learn that we are not left to find our way as best we can, and that God never expected that we should have any wisdom or competence in ourselves to walk according to His mind. The Lord could say, "Without Me ye can do nothing."

Thirdly, it is a very great day when we discover the rich provision that God has made in order that we might be intelligent in His mind. First, we have a Head in heaven—Christ in glory is the Head of His body, the Church—and all wisdom is in the Head, so that though we have no wisdom in ourselves we have full wisdom in Christ. One has truly said, "Christ is made wisdom to us, that is intelligence. He alone could lead men through the perplexities of this world of moral confusion, where there is no way." It is then of the first importance to give up our own "heads" and look to Christ as "the Head" to guide us. If we trust our own heads we are "not holding *the Head*" (Colossians 2:19).

Second, the Holy Spirit—a Divine Person—is on earth. The Lord knew well that His people would not be able to support themselves in a world from which He is absent; thus, before He left, He could say, "I will pray the Father, and He shall give you another Comforter, that He may abide with you for ever; even the Spirit of truth" (John 14:16-17). The preservation and maintenance of the truth is not dependent upon the saints, but upon the abiding presence of the Spirit of Truth.

Thirdly, we have the Holy Scriptures given by inspiration of God and profitable for doctrine, for reproof, for correction, for instruction in righteousness: that the man of God may be complete, thoroughly furnished unto all good works (2 Timothy 3:16-17). We read that "the house of God which is the assembly of the living God" is "the pillar and base of the truth"; but, when the house of God has become a ruin, and we no longer have the truth livingly set forth in the Church, the man of God still has the infallible authority of Scripture by which to prove all things.

Now it must be manifest that no ruin in Christendom can for one moment alter Christ, or the Spirit, or the Scriptures. Christ remains the Head in heaven, with boundless stores of wisdom for His people to draw upon, as much in these last days as in the first days of Christianity. The Holy Spirit abides with unabated power to guide and control. The Holy Scriptures remain with absolute authority.

Alas! Christendom has largely set aside Christ, the Spirit, and the Scriptures. The great religious systems of men have indeed retained the Name of Christ, but have set aside Christ as the Head in Heaven by appointing earthly heads. Rome has its Pope, the Greek Church its Patriarch, the Protestant Churches their Kings, Archbishops, Presidents or Moderators. Then in these great systems there is little left for the Spirit. The religious machinery and carnal devices of men have largely shut out the Spirit. And, lastly, men have made the most deadly attack upon the Scriptures, until there is hardly a sect in Christendom that holds with any degree of unanimity that "all Scripture is given by inspiration of God".

If, then, we desire to give Christ His place as the Head of the Church, to own and submit to the control of the Holy Spirit, and to implicitly bow to Scripture, what are we to do? Scripture very definitely answers that we must maintain and act upon two great principles. First *separation from all that is contrary to the truth of God*—all that is a denial of the truth of the Church, of Christ as the Head of His Church, of the Holy Spirit as our all-sufficient guide, and the Scriptures as our absolute authority. Then, having separated from evil, Scripture insists upon another equally important principle—*association with all that is according to God*. In a word, we must "Cease to do evil; learn to do well."

First, then, let us seek to learn what Scripture has to say as to *separation from evil*. All would admit, however much we may come short in practice, that separation from this evil world has ever been incumbent upon the people of God; but in a day when Christianity has become corrupted, we have special instructions for a three-fold separation. First, *separation from every religious system which by its constitution is a denial of the truth of Christ and the Church*. The word in Hebrews 13:13, is very plain, "Let us go forth therefore unto Him *without the camp*, bearing His reproach". The camp was the Jewish religious system originally set up by God and making its appeal to the natural man. In it no question of new birth was raised, all depended upon natural birth. It was composed of people outwardly in relationship with God, with an earthly order of priests who stood between the people and God. It had a worldly sanctuary and an ordered ritual (Hebrews 9:1-10). It is only too manifest that the religious systems of Christendom have been formed after the pattern of the camp. They are largely composed of unconverted men; they, too, make a definite appeal to the natural man; they, too, have their worldly sanctuaries, their ritual, and their humanly ordained priests that stand between the people and God. But alas! in imitating the camp, Christians, as we have seen, have set aside Christ as the Head, the Holy Spirit as Guide, and the Scriptures as authority. If, then, we would give Christ His true place we must, in obedience to the Word, "Go forth unto Him without the camp, bearing His reproach."

But, second, separation from the camp order of things as set forth in these religious systems is not enough. Scripture also plainly enjoins *separation from evil doctrine*. In the second chapter of the 2nd Epistle to Timothy and the 19th verse, we read, "Let every one that nameth the

Name of the Lord *depart from iniquity*." Every one who confesses the Name of the Lord is, by profession, identified with the Lord and is responsible to withdraw from iniquity. The iniquity may take many forms, but the preceding verses plainly show that evil doctrines are especially in view. We must not link iniquity with the Name of the Lord. It may cost us much in time to separate from iniquity, but it will cost us much more in eternity to link up the Name of the Lord with iniquity.

Thirdly, the same Scripture demands *separation from evil persons*. Verse 20 speaks of vessels to honour and to dishonour, and in the following verse we are enjoined to purge ourselves from the vessels to dishonour in order to be sanctified and meet for the Master's use. Here it is clear that persons are in view, not merely doctrines. It has been truly remarked: "It is always in proportion to your separation from these vessels—persons, not their doctrines merely, that you are sanctified and meet for the Master's use. ... Few have an idea how one suffers from unhallowed society. It is not enough not to hold their doctrines; but their society contaminates. You are coloured by the lowest company that you keep. Every effort has been tried in Christendom to weaken the force of this passage; every one is great in proportion to his separation."

Thus it is clear that Scripture plainly enjoins separation from religious systems that are a denial of the truth, from false doctrines that undermine the truth, and from vessels to dishonour who do not practice the truth.

This, however, is not enough. Separation, however necessary, is only negative, there must be also that which is positive. This leads us to the second great principle, *association with good*. Just as separation is to be from evil things as well as evil persons, so, too, the association is to be with things that are right and good as well as with persons who are right with the Lord. We are to "follow righteousness, faith, love, peace, with them that call on the Lord out of a pure heart" (2 Timothy 2:22). Righteousness of necessity stands first. Whatever profession a man may make, if there is not the maintenance of practical righteousness, there cannot be a walk according to God. But righteousness is not enough: mere right and wrong is not sufficient to determine the Christian's path. He must indeed do right, but to take the path of the Lord requires faith. Therefore with righteousness "faith" must be followed. But righteousness and faith make way for "love". If love is not guarded by righteousness and faith it will degenerate into mere human affection and be used as a plea for the allowance of laxity and the passing over of evil. Then these three qualities lead to "peace". Not a dishonourable peace that is only a compromise with evil, unbelief and hatred; but an honourable peace that is the outcome of righteousness, faith, and love. But if we follow these beautiful qualities we shall find others who are doing the same—those who call on the Lord out of a pure heart—and with such we are to associate. The fact that they call on the Lord out of a pure heart can plainly be discerned by their practical lives, inasmuch as it can be seen that they have "departed from iniquity", purged themselves from vessels to dishonour, and follow "righteousness, faith, love, peace". It is therefore clear that the path of separation is not a path of isolation. Scripture shows that there will always be those with whom we can associate.

However, those who, in the midst of the corruption of Christendom, take this path of separation from evil and association with good, will have raised against them "foolish and senseless questions" by those who oppose a path that they have not faith to take. To meet such it will be necessary to cultivate a spirit of "gentleness", "patience", and "meekness". Only as we wear this character will it be possible to avoid strife while seeking to instruct (2 Timothy 2:23-26).

It will be noticed that in these Scriptures that give such definite instruction for the people of God in a day of ruin, it is not once suggested that we should go outside the house of God. Indeed, to do so is impossible without going outside Christendom, which would involve leaving the world altogether. But while we cannot go outside the house, we are responsible to separate from the evil in the house. Again, we are not told to reconstruct anything. We are not told to rebuild the house. We are not called to form a pattern Church, or to start anything new. We are simply to walk in the light of that which was in the beginning, and which still exists under the eye of God in spite of all the failure of man in responsibility. That is to say, it is still our privilege and responsibility to walk in the truth of the Church, in the recognition of Christ as the Head, under the control and guidance of the Holy Spirit, and according to the instructions of Scripture.

www.ingramcontent.com/pod-product-compliance
Lightning Source LLC
Chambersburg PA
CBHW032148040426
42449CB00005B/448